ANARCHISM,
ANARCHIST COMMUNISM,
AND THE STATE

Revolutionary Pocketbooks

ANARCHISM, ANARCHIST COMMUNISM, AND THE STATE
THREE ESSAYS

Peter Kropotkin
Introduction by Brian Morris
Edited and with Bibliographic Notes by Iain McKay

Anarchism, Anarchist Communism, and The State: Three Essays
Peter Kropotkin
This edition copyright © 2019 PM Press
All rights reserved. No part of this book may be transmitted by any
means without permission in writing from the publisher.

ISBN: 978-1-62963-575-0
Library of Congress Control Number: 2018931533

Cover by John Yates/Stealworks
Layout by Jonathan Rowland based on work by briandesign

10 9 8 7 6 5 4 3 2 1

PM Press
PO Box 23912
Oakland, CA 94623
www.pmpress.org

Printed in the USA

■ CONTENTS

■ INTRODUCTION

BY BRIAN MORRIS

> *The present is where we get lost—if we forget our past and have*
> *no vision of the future.*

So wrote the Ghanaian poet Ayi Kwei Armah.

The anarchist geographer Peter Kropotkin is certainly a figure from our past that we should not forget. A talented geographer, a pioneer ecologist and a revolutionary socialist, Kropotkin generated a 'treasury of fertile ideas' (as his friend Errico Malatesta put it) that still have contemporary relevance. During his own lifetime, he was perhaps the most important and influential anarchist theoretician. Even the redoubtable Emma Goldman described Kropotkin as 'my teacher'.

Indeed, we need to stress that Kropotkin, like Michael Bakunin, is not just some historical curiosity or Russian relic of interest only to academic scholars, for his extraordinary life, his seminal writings, and his vision of a world free of political oppression and economic exploitation continue to be a source of inspiration and ideas—at least to evolutionary naturalists and libertarian socialists.

Born in Moscow in 1842, it is one of the curious ironies of history that Kropotkin, who became one of the fiercest opponents of all forms of State power, was born into the highest rank of the Russian aristocracy, for his princely forbears had been among the earliest rulers of Russia. Educated at an elite military academy, Kropotkin joined a newly formed Cossack regiment and spent his youthful years largely engaged in exploring and undertaking scientific research in the remote regions of

Manchuria and Siberia. His travels and research gave Kropotkin not only a keen sense of independence but established early his reputation as a unique and talented scientist—specifically in the field of physical geography. Kropotkin's portrait still hangs in the library of the Royal Geographic Society in London.

Having resolved not to devote his life purely to academic scholarship, Kropotkin took a sharp turn in 1872. On a visit to Zurich, Kropotkin became involved with the International Working Men's Association. Switzerland was then a Mecca of international socialism, a meeting place not only for Russian exiles, but also a refuge for many French socialists who had been involved in the Paris Commune of 1871. Kropotkin thus became an anarchist—a libertarian socialist.

Returning to St. Petersburg, Kropotkin joined a small group of revolutionary Narodniks (populists), the Chaikovsky Circle, and in 1874 was arrested for conspiring against the 'sacred person' of the Russian tsar. The two years Kropotkin spent imprisoned in the Peter and Paul Fortress and his subsequent dramatic escape are vividly described in Kropotkin's own autobiography *Memoirs of a Revolutionist* (1899).

During the years 1877 to 1882, Kropotkin travelled widely throughout Europe, engaged in anarchist propaganda and became deeply involved with the Jura Federation in Switzerland. Together with François Dumertheray, Élisée Reclus, Errico Malatesta, Carlo Cafiero and others, Kropotkin was instrumental in establishing anarchist communism (or libertarian socialism) as a political movement and tradition. Kropotkin always insisted that anarchist communism was not the creation of an intellectual elite but emerged from within the international working-class movement.

Inevitably, in 1883, Kropotkin was arrested in France for belonging to an illegal political organisation—the International Working Men's Association. He spent three years in Clairvaux Prison, to be finally released in January 1886. Like Marx before him, Kropotkin came to London and remained in Britain as an 'honourable exile' (as author Nicolas Walter described him) for the next thirty years, until his return to Russia after the 1917 revolution.

During his many years of exile, Kropotkin not only became the foremost theoretician of anarchism—and an inspiration to many socialists—but, as anthologist Iain McKay stresses, was always involved in concrete political struggles as a militant anarchist. During these same years, Kropotkin earned his living as a scientific journalist, as well as producing a steady stream of articles, pamphlets and books. They include, for example, specifically anarchist writings, such as *Words of a Rebel* (1885) and *The Conquest of Bread* (1892); studies in social ecology, *Fields, Factories and Workshops* (1895) and *Mutual Aid: A Factor in Evolution* (1902); and an impressive historical study, *The Great French Revolution* (1909), which so excited Lenin. Kropotkin was an extraordinarily well-read scholar who produced well-researched and lucidly and engagingly written books.

A 'true pioneer', as well as being a kind and amiable man, Kropotkin not only outlined the basic tenets of anarchist communism as a political tradition but expressed in embryonic form a new metaphysics of nature—evolutionary naturalism. Contemporary academics who dismiss Kropotkin as a 'mechanistic materialist' or 'positivist' simply fail to understand that Kropotkin was fundamentally a historical thinker, and following in the footsteps of Alexander von Humboldt and Charles Darwin—both kindred spirits—advocated a form of evolutionary naturalism—a metaphysic that stressed the importance of novelty, spontaneity, flux and self-organisation in the evolution of life on earth.

As is well-known, in 1914, to the surprise and dismay of his anarchist friends, Kropotkin supported the allies against Germany at the outbreak of the First World War, motivated, it seems, by an extreme antipathy towards German militarism. Most anarchists, including, for example, Malatesta, felt that Kropotkin had completely betrayed his anarchist principles.

Three years later, in declining health, Kropotkin returned to Russia, spending his last years writing a study of *Ethics* (1920). Kropotkin died in 1921, and around one hundred thousand people attended his funeral in Moscow. According to Victor Serge, this was the last major demonstration against Bolshevik tyranny. This pamphlet consists of three seminal articles by Peter Kropotkin, all written to appeal to the general reader. Together they provide an excellent introduction to anarchist communism.

Anarchism

This short article gives a succinct appraisal of the historical development of anarchism as a political tradition. Written in 1905, it first appeared in the 11th edition of the *Encyclopaedia Britannica* (1910) and has since been reprinted and translated many times.

Anarchist Communism: Its Basis and Principles

This essay brings together two separate articles, both published in 1887 in *The Nineteenth Century*, 'The Scientific Bases of Anarchy' (February) and 'The Coming Anarchy' (August). Together they provide an excellent summary of anarchist theory and the main principles of anarchist communism. First printed as a pamphlet by Freedom in 1891, it has since been reprinted many times.

The State: Its Historic Role

Intended as a lecture to be given in Paris in 1896 (Kropotkin was forbidden to enter France), it was first published in France the following year. An English translation appeared as a Freedom pamphlet in 1898. It gives a succinct account of human social evolution and the rise of the modern State from around 1600, as well as implicitly critiquing Marxist 'glorification of the State'. Like the other essays it has been reprinted many times over the years.

In an era when corporate capitalism reigns triumphant, creating conditions that induce fear, social dislocations, gross economic inequalities and political and ecological crises, and when there is a pervasive mood of 'apocalyptic despair' among many intellectuals (and some anarchists) there is surely a need to take seriously Kropotkin's vision of an alternative way of organising social life. These three essays support and articulate that vision.

■ ANARCHISM

Anarchism (from the Greek άν- [*an-*], and άρχή [*archos*], contrary to authority), the name given to a principle or theory of life and conduct under which society is conceived without government—harmony in such a society being obtained, not by submission to law, or by obedience to any authority, but by free agreements concluded between the various groups, territorial and professional, freely constituted for the sake of production and consumption, as also for the satisfaction of the infinite variety of needs and aspirations of a civilised being. In a society developed on these lines, the voluntary associations which already now begin to cover all the fields of human activity would take a still greater extension so as to substitute themselves for the State in all its functions. They would represent an interwoven network, composed of an infinite variety of groups and federations of all sizes and degrees, local, regional, national and international—temporary or more or less permanent—for all possible purposes: production, consumption and exchange, communications, sanitary arrangements, education, mutual protection, defence of the territory and so on; and, on the other side, for the satisfaction of an ever-increasing number of scientific, artistic, literary and sociable needs. Moreover, such a society would represent nothing immutable. On the contrary—as is seen in organic life at large—harmony would (it is contended) result from an ever-changing adjustment and readjustment of equilibrium between the multitudes of forces and influences, and this adjustment would be the easier to obtain as none of the forces would enjoy a special protection from the State.

If, it is contended, society were organised on these principles, man would not be limited in the free exercise of his powers
in productive work by a capitalist monopoly, maintained by the
State; nor would he be limited in the exercise of his will by a
fear of punishment, or by obedience towards individuals or
metaphysical entities, which both lead to depression of initiative and servility of mind. He would be guided in his actions
by his own understanding, which necessarily would bear the
impression of a free action and reaction between his own self
and the ethical conceptions of his surroundings. Man would
thus be enabled to obtain the full development of all his facul-
ties, intellectual, artistic and moral, without being hampered by
overwork for the monopolists, or by the servility and inertia of
mind of the great number. He would thus be able to reach full
individualisation, which is not possible either under the present
system of *individualism*, or under any system of State Socialism
in the so-called *Volkstaat* (popular State).

The Anarchist writers consider, moreover, that their conception is not a Utopia, constructed on the *a priori* method, after
a few desiderata have been taken as postulates. It is derived,
they maintain, from an *analysis of tendencies* that are at work
already, even though State Socialism may find a temporary
favour with the reformers. The progress of modern technics,
which wonderfully simplifies the production of all the necessaries of life; the growing spirit of independence, and the rapid
spread of free initiative and free understanding in all branches
of activity—including those which formerly were considered
as the proper attribution of Church and State—are steadily
reinforcing the no-government tendency.

As to their economical conceptions, the Anarchists, in
common with all Socialists, of whom they constitute the left
wing, maintain that the now prevailing system of private ownership in land, and our capitalist production for the sake of
profits, represent a monopoly which runs against both the principles of justice and the dictates of utility. They are the main

obstacle which prevents the successes of modern technics from being brought into the service of all, so as to produce general well-being. The Anarchists consider the wage system and capitalist production altogether as an obstacle to progress. But they point out also that the State was, and continues to be, the chief instrument for permitting the few to monopolise the land, and the capitalists to appropriate for themselves a quite disproportionate share of the yearly accumulated surplus of production. Consequently, while combating the present monopolisation of land, and capitalism altogether, the Anarchists combat with the same energy the State, as the main support of that system. Not this or that special form, but the State altogether, whether it be a monarchy or even a republic governed by means of the *referendum*.

The State organisation, having always been, both in ancient and modern history (Macedonian Empire, Roman Empire, modern European States grown up on the ruins of the autonomous cities), the instrument for establishing monopolies in favour of the ruling minorities cannot be made to work for the destruction of these monopolies. The Anarchists consider, therefore, that to hand over to the State all the main sources of economical life—the land, the mines, the railways, banking, insurance and so on—as also the management of all the main branches of industry, in addition to all the functions already accumulated in its hands (education, State-supported religions, defence of the territory, etc.), would mean to create a new instrument of tyranny. State capitalism would only increase the powers of bureaucracy and capitalism. True progress lies in the direction of decentralisation, both *territorial* and *functional*, in the development of the spirit of local and personal initiative, and of free federation from the simple to the compound, *in lieu* of the present hierarchy from the centre to the periphery.

In common with most Socialists, the Anarchists recognise that, like all evolution in nature, the slow evolution of society

9

is followed from time to time by periods of accelerated evolution which are called revolutions; and they think that the era of revolutions is not yet closed. Periods of rapid changes will follow the periods of slow evolution, and these periods must be taken advantage of—not for increasing and widening the powers of the State, but for reducing them, through the organisation in every township or commune of the local groups of producers and consumers, as also the regional, and eventually the international, federations of these groups.

In virtue of the above principles the Anarchists refuse to be party to the present State organisation and to support it by infusing fresh blood into it. They do not seek to constitute, and invite the working men not to constitute, political parties in the parliaments. Accordingly, since the foundation of the International Working Men's Association in 1864–1866, they have endeavoured to promote their ideas directly amongst the labour organisations and to induce those unions to a direct struggle against capital, without placing their faith in parliamentary legislation.

1. The Historical Development of Anarchism

The conception of society just sketched, and the tendency which is its dynamic expression, have always existed in mankind, in opposition to the governing hierarchic conception and tendency—now the one and now the other taking the upper hand at different periods of history. To the former tendency we owe the evolution, by the masses themselves, of those institutions—the clan, the village community, the guild, the free medieval city—by means of which the masses resisted the encroachments of the conquerors and the power-seeking minorities. The same tendency asserted itself with great energy in the great religious movements of medieval times, especially in the early movements of the reform and its forerunners. At the same time, it evidently found its expression in the writings of some thinkers, since the times of Lao-Tzu, although, owing to its non-scholastic and popular origin, it obviously found less sympathy among the scholars than the opposed tendency.

As has been pointed out by Prof. Adler in his *Geschichte des Sozialismus und Kommunismus*, Aristippus (born c. 430 BCE), one of the founders of the Cyrenaic school, already taught that the wise must not give up their liberty to the State, and in reply to a question by Socrates he said that he did not desire to belong either to the governing or the governed class. Such an attitude, however, seems to have been dictated merely by an Epicurean attitude towards the life of the masses.

The best exponent of Anarchist philosophy in ancient Greece was Zeno (342–267 or 270 BCE), from Crete, the founder of the Stoic philosophy, who distinctly opposed his conception of a free community without government to the State Utopia of Plato. He repudiated the omnipotence of the State, its intervention and regimentation, and proclaimed the sovereignty of the moral law of the individual—remarking already that, while the necessary instinct of self-preservation leads man to egotism, nature has supplied a corrective to it by providing man with another instinct—that of sociability. When men are reasonable enough to follow their natural instincts, they will unite across the frontiers and constitute the cosmos. They will have no need of law-courts or police, will have no temples and no public worship, and use no money—free gifts taking the place of the exchanges. Unfortunately, the writings of Zeno have not reached us and are only known through fragmentary quotations. However, the fact that his very wording is similar to the wording now in use, shows how deeply is laid the tendency of human nature of which he was the mouthpiece.

In medieval times we find the same views on the State expressed by the illustrious bishop of Alba, Marco Girolamo Vida, in his first dialogue *De dignitate reipublicae* (Ferd. Cavalli, in *Mem. dell'Istituto Veneto*, xiii.; Dr. E. Nys, *Researches in the History of Economics*). But it is especially in several early Christian movements, beginning with the ninth century in Armenia, and in the preachings of the early Hussites, particularly Chojecki, and the early Anabaptists, especially Hans Denck (cf. Keller, *Ein Apostel der Wiedertäufer*), that one finds the same ideas forcibly expressed—special stress being laid of course on their moral aspects.

Rabelais and Fénelon, in their Utopias, have also expressed similar ideas, and they were also current in the eighteenth century amongst the French Encyclopaedists, as may be concluded from separate expressions occasionally met with in the writings of Rousseau, from Diderot's "Preface" to the *Voyage* of Bougainville and so on. However, in all probability such ideas could not be developed then, owing to the rigorous censorship of the Roman Catholic Church.

These ideas found their expression later during the Great French Revolution. While the Jacobins did all in their power to centralise everything in the hands of the government, it appears now, from recently published documents, that the masses of the people, in their municipalities and 'sections', accomplished a considerable constructive work. They appropriated for themselves the election of the judges, the organisation of supplies and equipment for the army, as also for the large cities, work for the unemployed, the management of charities and so on. They even tried to establish a direct correspondence between the 36,000 communes of France through the intermediary of a special board, outside the National Assembly (cf. Sigismund Lacroix, *Actes de la commune de Paris*).

It was Godwin, in his *Enquiry Concerning Political Justice* (2 vols., 1793), who was the first to formulate the political and economical conceptions of Anarchism, even though he did not give that name to the ideas developed in his remarkable work. Laws, he wrote, are not a product of the wisdom of our ancestors: they are the product of their passions, their timidity, their jealousies and their ambition. The remedy they offer is worse than the evils they pretend to cure. If and only if all laws and courts were abolished, and the decisions in the arising contests were left to reasonable men chosen for that purpose, real justice would gradually be evolved. As to the State, Godwin frankly claimed its abolition. A society, he wrote, can perfectly well exist without any government: only the communities should be small and perfectly autonomous. Speaking of property, he stated that the rights of everyone 'to every substance capable of contributing to the benefit of a human being' must be regulated by justice alone: the substance must go 'to him who most wants it'. His conclusion was Communism. Godwin, however, had not the courage to maintain his opinions. He entirely rewrote later on his chapter on property and mitigated his Communist views in the second edition of *Political Justice* (8 vols., 1796).

Proudhon was the first to use, in 1840 (*Qu'est-ce que la propriété?* first memoir), the name of Anarchy with application to the no-government state of society. The name of 'Anarchists' had been freely applied during the French Revolution by the Girondists to those revolutionaries who did not consider that the task of the Revolution was accomplished with the overthrow of Louis XVI, and insisted upon a series of economical measures being taken (the abolition of feudal rights without redemption, the return to the village communities of the communal lands enclosed since 1669, the limitation of landed property to 120 acres, progressive income tax, the national organisation of exchanges on a just value basis, which already received a beginning of practical realisation and so on).

Now Proudhon advocated a society without government, and used the word Anarchy to describe it. Proudhon repudiated, as is known, all schemes of Communism, according to which mankind would be driven into communistic monasteries or barracks, as also all the schemes of State or State-aided Socialism which were advocated by Louis Blanc and the Collectivists. When he proclaimed in his first memoir on property that 'property is theft', he meant only property in its present, Roman-law, sense of 'right of use and abuse'; in property-rights, on the other hand, understood in the limited sense of *possession*, he saw the best protection against the encroachments of the State. At the same time he did not want violently to dispossess the present owners of land, dwelling-houses, mines, factories and so on. He preferred to attain the same end by rendering capital incapable of earning interest; and this he proposed to obtain by means of a national bank, based on the mutual confidence of all those who are engaged in production, who would agree to exchange among themselves their produces at cost-value, by means of labour cheques representing the hours of labour required to produce every given commodity. Under such a system, which Proudhon described as '*Mutuellisme*', all the exchanges of services would be strictly equivalent. Besides, such a bank would be enabled to lend money without interest, levying only something like 1 per cent, or even less, for covering the cost of administration. Everyone being thus enabled to borrow the money that would be required to buy a house, nobody would agree to pay any more a yearly rent for the use of it. A general 'social liquidation' would thus be rendered easy, without violent expropriation. The same applied to mines, railways, factories and so on.

In a society of this type the State would be useless. The chief relations between citizens would be based on free agreement and regulated by mere account keeping. The contests might be settled by arbitration. A penetrating criticism of the State and all possible forms of government, and a deep insight into all economic problems, were well-known characteristics of Proudhon's work.

It is worth noticing that French mutualism had its precursor in England, in William Thompson, who began by mutualism before he became a Communist, and in his followers John Gray (*A Lecture on Human Happiness*, 1825; *The Social System*, 1831) and J.F. Bray (*Labour's Wrongs and Labour's Remedy*, 1839). It had also its precursor in America. Josiah Warren, who was born in 1798 (cf. W. Bailie, *Josiah Warren, the First American Anarchist*, Boston, 1900) and belonged to Owen's 'New Harmony', considered that the failure of this enterprise was chiefly due to the suppression of individuality and the lack of initiative and responsibility. These defects, he taught, were inherent to every scheme based upon authority and the community of goods. He advocated, therefore, complete individual liberty. In 1827 he opened in Cincinnati a little country store which was the first 'Equity Store', and which the people called 'Time Store', because it was based on labour being exchanged hour for hour in all sorts of produce. 'Cost—the limit of price', and consequently 'no interest', was the motto of his store, and later on of his 'Equity Village', near New York, which was still in existence in 1865. Mr. Keith's 'House of Equity' at Boston, founded in 1855, is also worthy of notice.

While the economical, and especially the mutual-banking, ideas of Proudhon found supporters and even a practical application in the United States, his political conception of Anarchy found but little echo in France, where the Christian Socialism of Lamennais and the Fourierists, and the State Socialism of Louis Blanc and the followers of Saint-Simon, were dominating. These ideas found, however, some temporary support among the left-wing Hegelians in Germany, Moses Hess in 1843, and Karl Grün in 1845, who advocated Anarchism. Besides, the authoritarian Communism of Wilhelm Weitling having given origin to opposition amongst the Swiss working men, Wilhelm Marr gave expression to it in the [eighteen] forties.

On the other side, Individualist Anarchism found, also in Germany, its fullest expression in Max Stirner ([Johann] Kaspar Schmidt), whose remarkable works (*Der Einzige und sein Eigentum* and articles contributed to the *Rheinische Zeitung*) remained quite overlooked until they were brought into prominence by John Henry Mackay.

Prof. V. Basch, in a very able introduction to his interesting book, *L'individualisme anarchiste: Max Stirner* (1904), has shown how the development of the German philosophy from Kant to Hegel, and 'the absolute' of Schelling and the *Geist* of Hegel, necessarily provoked, when the anti-Hegelian revolt began, the preaching of the same 'absolute' in the camp of the rebels. This was done by Stirner, who advocated, not only a complete revolt against the State and against the servitude which authoritarian Communism would impose upon men, but also the full liberation of the individual from all social and moral bonds—the rehabilitation of the 'I', the supremacy of the individual, complete 'amoralism', and the 'association of the egotists'. The final conclusion of that sort of Individual Anarchism has been indicated by Prof. Basch. It maintains that the aim of all superior civilisation is, not to permit *all* members of the community to develop in a normal way, but to permit certain better endowed individuals 'fully to develop', even at the cost of the happiness and the very existence of the mass of mankind. It is thus a return towards the most common individualism, advocated by all the would-be superior minorities, to which indeed man owes in his history precisely the State and the rest, which these individualists combat. Their individualism goes so far as to end in a negation of their own starting point,—to say nothing of the impossibility for the individual to attain a really full development in the conditions of oppression of the masses by the 'beautiful aristocracies'. His development would remain unilateral. This is why this direction of thought, notwithstanding its undoubtedly correct and useful advocacy of the full development of each individuality, finds a hearing only in limited artistic and literary circles.

2. Anarchism in the International Working Men's Association

A general depression in the propaganda of all fractions of Socialism followed, as is known, after the defeat of the uprising of the Paris working men in June 1848 and the fall of the Republic. All the Socialist press was gagged during the reaction period, which lasted fully twenty years. Nevertheless, even Anarchist thought began to make some progress, namely in the writings of Bellegarrigue (Caeurderoy), and especially

Joseph Déjacque (*Les Lazaréennes*, *L'Humanisphère*, an Anarchist-Communist Utopia, lately discovered and reprinted). The Socialist movement revived only after 1864, when some French working men, all 'mutualists', meeting in London during the Universal Exhibition with English followers of Robert Owen, founded the International Working Men's Association. This association developed very rapidly and adopted a policy of direct economical struggle against capitalism, without interfering in the political parliamentary agitation, and this policy was followed until 1871. However, after the Franco-German War, when the International Association was prohibited in France after the uprising of the Commune, the German working men, who had received manhood suffrage for elections to the newly constituted imperial parliament, insisted upon modifying the tactics of the International, and began to build up a Social-Democratic political party. This soon led to a division in the Working Men's Association, and the Latin federations, Spanish, Italian, Belgian and Jurassic (France could not be represented), constituted among themselves a Federal union which broke entirely with the Marxist general council of the International. Within these federations developed now what may be described as *modern Anarchism*. After the names of 'Federalists' and 'Anti-authoritarians' had been used for some time by these federations the name of 'Anarchists', which their adversaries insisted upon applying to them, prevailed, and finally it was revindicated.

Bakunin soon became the leading spirit among these Latin federations for the development of the principles of Anarchism, which he did in a number of writings, pamphlets and letters. He demanded the complete abolition of the State, which—he wrote—is a product of religion, belongs to a lower state of civilisation, represents the negation of liberty, and spoils even that which it undertakes to do for the sake of general well-being. The State was an historically necessary evil, but its complete extinction will be, sooner or later, equally necessary.

Repudiating all legislation, even when issuing from universal suffrage, Bakunin claimed for each nation, each region and each commune, full autonomy, so long as it is not a menace to its neighbours, and full independence for the individual, adding that one becomes really free only when, and in proportion as, all others are free. Free federations of the communes would constitute free nations.

As to his economical conceptions, Bakunin described himself, in common with his Federalist comrades of the International (César de Paepe, James Guillaume, [Adhémar] Schwitzguébel), a 'Collectivist Anarchist'—not in the sense of Vidal and Pecqueur in the 1840s, or of their modern Social-Democratic followers, but to express a state of things in which all necessaries for production are owned in common by the Labour groups and the free communes, while the ways of retribution of labour, Communist or otherwise, would be settled by each group for itself. Social revolution, the near approach of which was foretold at that time by all Socialists, would be the means of bringing into life the new conditions.

The Jurassic, the Spanish, and the Italian federations and sections of the International Working Men's Association, as also the French, the German and the American Anarchist groups, were for the next years the chief centres of Anarchist thought and propaganda. They refrained from any participation in parliamentary politics, and always kept in close contact with the labour organisations. However, in the second half of the eighties and the early nineties of the nineteenth century, when the influence of the Anarchists began to be felt in strikes, in the 1st of May demonstrations, where they promoted the idea of a general strike for an eight-hour day, and in the anti-militarist propaganda in the army, violent prosecutions were directed against them, especially in the Latin countries (including physical torture in the Barcelona Castle) and the United States (the execution of five Chicago Anarchists in 1887). Against these prosecutions the Anarchists retaliated by acts of violence which in their turn were followed by more executions from above, and new acts of revenge from below. This created in the general public the impression that violence is the substance of Anarchism, a view repudiated by its supporters, who hold that in reality violence is resorted to by all parties in proportion as their open action is obstructed by repression, and exceptional laws render them outlaws (cf. *Anarchism and Outrage*, by C.M. Wilson, and *Report of the Spanish Atrocities Committee*, in 'Freedom Pamphlets'; *A Concise History of the Great Trial of the Chicago Anarchists*, by Dyer Lum [New York, 1886]; *The Chicago Martyrs: Speeches*, etc.).

Anarchism continued to develop, partly in the direction of Proudhonian 'Mutuellisme', but chiefly as Communist-Anarchism, to which a third direction, Christian-Anarchism, was added by Leo Tolstoy, and a fourth, which might be ascribed as literary-Anarchism, began amongst some prominent modern writers.

The ideas of Proudhon, especially as regards mutual banking, corresponding with those of Josiah Warren, found a considerable following in the United States, creating quite a school, of which the main writers are Stephen Pearl Andrews, William Greene, Lysander Spooner (who began to write in 1850, and whose unfinished work, *Natural Law*, was full of promise), and several others, whose names will be found in Dr. Nettlau's *Bibliographie de l'anarchie*.

A prominent position among the Individualist Anarchists in America has been occupied by Benjamin R. Tucker, whose journal *Liberty* was started in 1881 and whose conceptions are a combination of those of Proudhon with those of Herbert Spencer. Starting from the statement that Anarchists are egotists, strictly speaking, and that every group of individuals, be it a secret league of a few persons or the Congress of the United States, has the right to oppress all mankind, provided it has the power to do so, that equal liberty for all and absolute equality ought to be the law, and 'mind everyone your own business' is the unique moral law of Anarchism, Tucker goes on to prove that a general and thorough application of these principles would be beneficial and would offer no danger, because the powers of every individual would be limited by the exercise of the equal rights of all others. He further indicated (following H. Spencer) the difference which exists between the encroachment on somebody's rights and resistance to such an encroachment; between domination and defence: the former being equally condemnable, whether it be encroachment of a criminal upon an individual, or the encroachment of one upon all others, or of all others upon one; while resistance to encroachment is defensible and necessary. For their self-defence, both the citizen and the group have the right to any violence, including capital punishment. Violence is also justified for enforcing the duty of keeping an agreement. Tucker thus follows Spencer and, like him, opens (in the present writer's opinion) the way for reconstituting under the heading of 'defence' all the functions of the State. His criticism of the present State is very searching, and his defence of the rights of the individual very powerful. As regards his economical views, B.R. Tucker follows Proudhon.

The Individualist Anarchism of the American Proudhonians finds, however, but little sympathy amongst the working masses. Those who profess it—they are chiefly 'intellectuals'—soon realise that the *individualisation* they so highly praise is not attainable by individual efforts, and either abandon the ranks of the Anarchists and are driven into the Liberal individualism of the classical economist, or they retire into a sort of Epicurean amoralism or superman theory, similar to that of Stirner and Nietzsche. The great bulk of the Anarchist working men prefer the Anarchist-Communist ideas which have gradually evolved out of the Anarchist Collectivism of the International Working Men's Association. To this direction belong—to name only the better-known exponents of Anarchism—Élisée Reclus, Jean Grave, Sébastien Faure, Émile Pouget in France; Errico Malatesta and Covelli in Italy; R. Mella,

A. Lorenzo and the mostly unknown authors of many excellent manifestos in Spain; John Most amongst the Germans; Spies, Parsons and their followers in the United States and so on; while [Ferdinand] Domela Nieuwenhuis occupies an intermediate position in Holland. The chief Anarchist papers which have been published since 1880 also belong to that direction; while a number of Anarchists of this direction have joined the so-called Syndicalist movement—the French name for the non-political Labour movement, devoted to direct struggle with capitalism, which has lately become so prominent in Europe.

As one of the Anarchist Communist direction, the present writer for many years endeavoured to develop the following ideas: to show the intimate, logical connection which exists between the modern philosophy of natural sciences and Anarchism; to put Anarchism on a scientific basis by the study of the tendencies that are apparent now in society and may indicate its further evolution; and to work out the basis of Anarchist ethics. As regards the substance of Anarchism itself, it was Kropotkin's aim to prove that Communism—at least partial—has more chances of being established than Collectivism, especially in communes taking the lead, and that Free, or Anarchist, Communism is the only form of Communism that has any chance of being accepted in civilised societies; Communism and Anarchy are therefore two terms of evolution which complete each other, the one rendering the other possible and acceptable. He has tried, moreover, to indicate how, during a revolutionary period, a large city—if its inhabitants have accepted the idea—could organise itself on the lines of Free Communism; the city guaranteeing to every inhabitant dwelling, food and clothing to an extent corresponding to the comfort now available to the middle classes only, in exchange for a half-day's, or five-hours', work; and how all those things which would be considered as luxuries might be obtained by everyone if he joins for the other half of the day all sorts of free associations pursuing all possible aims—educational, literary, scientific, artistic, sports and so on.

In order to prove the first of these assertions he has analysed the possibilities of agriculture and industrial work, both being combined with brain work. And in order to elucidate the main factors of human evolution, he has analysed the part played in history by the popular constructive agencies of mutual aid and the historical role of the State.

Without naming himself an Anarchist, Leo Tolstoy, like his predecessors in the popular religious movements of the fifteenth and sixteenth centuries, Chojecki, Denck and many others, took the Anarchist position as regards the State and property rights, deducing his conclusions from the general spirit of the teachings of the Christ and from the necessary dictates of reason. With all the might of his talent he made (especially in *The Kingdom of God Is Within You*) a powerful criticism of the Church, the State and law altogether, and especially of the present property laws. He describes the State as the domination of the wicked ones, supported by brutal force. Robbers, he says, are far less dangerous than a well-organised government. He makes a searching criticism of the prejudices which are current now concerning the benefits conferred upon men by the Church, the State and the existing distribution of property, and from the teachings of the Christ he deduces the rule of non-resistance and the absolute condemnation of all wars. His religious arguments are, however, so well combined with arguments borrowed from a dispassionate observation of the present evils, that the Anarchist portions of his works appeal to the religious and the non-religious reader alike.

It would be impossible to represent here, in a short sketch, the penetration, on the one hand, of Anarchist ideas into modern literature, and the influence, on the other hand, which the libertarian ideas of the best contemporary writers have exercised upon the development of Anarchism. One ought to consult the ten big volumes of the *Supplément Littéraire* to the paper *La Révolte* and later the *Temps Nouveaux*, which contain reproductions from the works of hundreds of modern authors expressing Anarchist ideas, in order to realise how closely Anarchism is connected with all the intellectual movement of our own times. J.S. Mill's *Liberty*, Spencer's *Individual versus The State*, [Jean-Marie] Guyau's *Morality without Obligation or Sanction*, and Fouillée's *La morale, l'art et la religion*, the works of Multatuli (E. Douwes Dekker), Richard Wagner's *Art and Revolution*, the works of Nietzsche, Emerson, W. Lloyd Garrison, Thoreau, Alexander Herzen, Edward Carpenter and so on; and in the domain of fiction, the dramas of Ibsen, the poetry of Walt Whitman, Tolstoy's *War and Peace*, Zola's *Paris* and *Le Travail*, the latest works of Merezhkovsky and an infinity of works of less known authors are full of ideas which show how closely Anarchism is interwoven with the work that is going on in modern thought in the same direction of enfranchisement of man from the bonds of the State as well as from those of capitalism.

■ IAIN MCKAY'S BIBLIOGRAPHICAL NOTES TO 'ANARCHISM'

As well as being an internationally known anarchist thinker, Kropotkin was also a scientist of renown, having made significant contributions to the understanding of the geography of Russia in the 1860s. He made regular contributions to the *Geographical Journal* and wrote on scientific issues for *The Nineteenth Century*, including a regular column on 'Recent Science' from 1892 to 1902. Unsurprisingly, as a leading expert on the subject, he was asked to provide or collaborate on many entries in the 11th edition of the *Encyclopaedia Britannica* relating to the geography, culture and politics of Russia.

More famously, however, he also contributed the entry on anarchism in that edition. Written in 1905, it was finally published in 1910 and was quickly recognised as a classic account of the ideas and history of anarchism. It has been reprinted as an anarchist pamphlet in its own right in many languages and rightly appears in many anthologies of Kropotkin's works, including *Direct Struggle Against Capital* (Edinburgh: AK Press, 2014) and *Anarchism: A Collection of Revolutionary Writings* (Mineola, NY: Dover Books, 2003). It continued to appear in the *Encyclopaedia Britannica* until 1960 edition, supplemented by postscripts in the 1927 and 1957 editions.

There is very little to add here, beyond stressing that while Kropotkin indicates the many thinkers and movements that expressed anarchist ideas before the word 'anarchist' was used by Proudhon in a positive sense in *What is Property?* (1840), he is also very clear that modern anarchism was born in the International Working Men's Association. Kropotkin wrote often of the International in anarchist newspapers, clearly recognising its key role in the development of anarchism, as well as considering it an ideal for the labour movement, being, as he repeatedly stressed, based on the direct struggle of labour against capital. He revisited the history of anarchism in the second expanded edition of *Modern Science and Anarchism* (1912), a revised and larger version of this being included as the first section of *La science moderne et l'anarchie* (1913).[1] There, being less restricted by the norms of academia, he emphasised the origin of anarchist ideas in the struggles of the oppressed and discussed the birth of anarchism itself in the First International in more detail.

Rather than ancient Greeks or obscure philosophers, the main influences in the birth of anarchism in the nineteenth century were the failure of the French Revolution to produce 'Liberty, Equality and Fraternity', the rise of capitalism and oppositional movements against it, namely, utopian socialism and the labour movement. And this is important, for anarchism as both a theory and a movement—regardless of the claims of some who seem only to have read a dictionary—has never been only against the State. As Kropotkin stresses, it has always opposed the authority produced by inequality and the accumulated property that goes with it. Anarchism, then, has always been part of the wider socialist movement, its libertarian or left wing as Kropotkin puts it here.[2] The likes of Proudhon, Bakunin

---

1   This book, the last published during Kropotkin's lifetime, was fully translated 105 years after the French edition; Iain McKay, ed., *Modern Science and Anarchy* (Edinburgh: AK Press, 2018).

2   Sadly, it is necessary to explain what we mean by 'libertarian', as this term has been appropriated by the free-market capitalist right. Socialist use of libertarian dates from 1857, when it was first used as a synonym for anarchist by communist-anarchist Joseph Déjacque in an 'Open Letter to Pierre-Joseph Proudhon', and in the following year

and Tucker all—like Kropotkin—called themselves socialists and opposed the exploitation of labour as much as oppression by the State, even if they disagreed on how best to end both.

Given this, it is important to remember that earlier anarchistic thinkers and movements were only considered as forerunners of anarchism after anarchism itself became a named socio-economic theory and movement. Likewise, libertarian movements and ideas can and have developed independently of the anarchist tradition after it was formed—indeed, most popular revolts have expressed anarchistic elements whether self-identified anarchists were present or not.

So libertarian trends have repeatedly appeared independently of anarchism, before and after 1840. This is unsurprising, though, for it would stagger belief that people living under the oppression of the State and property did not come to the conclusion that both had to be ended. However, it was Proudhon who provided a name for this perspective and the International that created a wide-scale enduring movement. That these thinkers and movements could retrospectively be called anarchist does not mean that they influenced Proudhon—particularly if he were unaware of them and they of him!

This relates to another aspect of anarchism which Kropotkin stresses here and in many other works, namely, that anarchists do not abstractly compare an ideal society to the grim reality of capitalism. Instead, we look to tendencies within capitalism that point beyond it—a methodology first utilised by Proudhon, as Kropotkin noted in his pamphlet *Revolutionary Studies* (1892). The labour movement, militant trade unionism, took pride of place in these tendencies and was seen as both a means of struggling against capitalism and as providing the

---

as the title for his paper *Le Libertaire, Journal du Mouvement Social*. This usage became more commonplace in the 1880s, and 1895 saw leading anarchists Sébastien Faure and Louise Michel publish *Le Libertaire* in France; see my '160 Years of Libertarian', *Anarcho-Syndicalist Review* no. 71 (Fall 2017).

structures which would replace it. In short, the struggle for freedom would create the forms of freedom, whether in the community or in the workplace.

The text included here is the one that was published in 1910—barring some minor corrections of spelling and the like. The text has been left to speak for itself, rather than burden it with footnotes, as befits an entry in an *Encyclopaedia*.[3] It does not, however, include the quite substantial footnote the editors felt obliged to add on 'a certain class of murderous outrages' in order to provide the reader a '*résumé* of the so-called "anarchist' incidents"' where they 'would expect to find them'. In addition, a lengthy bibliography of then current works and newspapers has also been excluded.

Although an excellent short and objective account of anarchism, it does contain some commonplace errors: Proudhon, regardless of the much repeated assertion otherwise, did not advocate 'labour notes' (pricing goods by the time taken to create them);[4] the British socialists Bray and Gray were advocates of central planning not mutualism or any other form of market socialism; Tucker did not support all aspects of Proudhon's economic ideas, embracing his ideas on banking, interest and landownership, while ignoring the arguments for workers' associations, socialisation, agricultural-industrial federation and so on.[5] However, in the main, it is a reliable

---

3   Various factual notes could easily be added. For example, Max Stirner's work *Der Einzige und sein Eigentum*—literally *The Unique and His Property*—was translated in 1907 by the American individualist anarchist Steven T. Byington (1869–1957), who decided to entitle it book *The Ego and Its Own*, and it is by this title it is best known in the English-speaking world.

4   Iain McKay, 'Proudhon's constituted value and the myth of labour notes', *Anarchist Studies*, Vol. 25, no. 1 (Spring 2017); Iain McKay, 'The Poverty of (Marx's) Philosophy', *Anarcho-Syndicalist Review* no. 70 (Summer 2017).

5   See my introduction to Pierre-Joseph Proudhon, *Property is Theft! A Pierre-Joseph Proudhon Anthology* (Edinburgh: AK Press, 2011).

account of anarchism, its ideas, its history and its tendencies. Unsurprisingly, it reflects Kropotkin's communist anarchist position, but as this was the perspective of the bulk of anarchists at the time (as now) this simply adds to its objectivity.

■ ANARCHIST COMMUNISM: ITS BASIS AND PRINCIPLES (1891)

Anarchy, the No-Government system of Socialism, has a double origin. It is an outgrowth of the two great movements of thought in the economical and the political fields which characterise our century, and especially its second part. In common with all Socialists, the Anarchists hold that the private ownership of land, capital and machinery has had its time; that it is condemned to disappear; and that all requisites for production must, and will, become the common property of society and be managed in common by the producers of wealth. And, in common with the most advanced representatives of political Radicalism, they maintain that the ideal of the political organisation of society is a condition of things where the functions of government are reduced to a minimum and the individual recovers his full liberty of initiative and action for satisfying, by means of free groups and federations—freely constituted— all the infinitely varied needs of the human being. As regards Socialism, most of the Anarchists arrive at its ultimate conclusion, that is, at a complete negation of the wage system and at Communism. And with reference to political organisation, by giving a further development to the above-mentioned part of the Radical programme, they arrive at the conclusion that the ultimate aim of society is the reduction of the functions of government to *nil*—that is, to a society without government, to An-archy. The Anarchists maintain, moreover, that such being the ideal of social and political organisation, they must not remit it to future centuries, but that only those changes in our social organisation which are in accordance with the above double ideal and constitute an approach to it will have a chance of life and be beneficial for the commonwealth.

As to the method followed by the Anarchist thinker, it entirely differs from that followed by the Utopists.[1] The Anarchist thinker does not resort to metaphysical conceptions (like 'natural rights', the 'duties of the State' and so on) to establish what are, in his opinion, the best conditions for realising the greatest happiness of humanity. He follows, on the contrary, the course traced by the modern philosophy of evolution—without entering, however, the slippery route of mere analogies so often resorted to by Herbert Spencer.[2] He studies human society as it is now and was in the past; and, without either endowing men altogether, or separate individuals, with superior qualities which they do not possess, he merely considers society as an aggregation of organisms trying to find out the best ways of combining the wants of the individual with those of co-operation for the welfare of the species. He studies

---

1   A reference to utopian socialists like Robert Owen and Charles Fourier, who presented detailed plans of a better system. Proudhon in *System of Economic Contradictions* (1846) argued that instead of contrasting visions of ideal communities to the grim reality of capitalism as they did, we had to analyse the system and explore its contradictions in order to identify those elements which appear within it which express the future. Thus, it was a case of 'studying, as Proudhon has already advised, the *tendencies* of society today and so forecasting the society of tomorrow'; Peter Kropotkin, *Revolutionary Studies* (London: The Commonweal, 1892), 12.

2   Herbert Spencer (1820–1903) was a prominent English classical liberal political theorist of the Victorian era, best known now for coining the term 'survival of the fittest'. He developed an all-embracing conception of evolution as progressive development in biology and society (*Synthetic Philosophy*), writing on ethics, religion, anthropology, economics, political theory, philosophy, biology, sociology and psychology. He was opposed to all forms of State intervention in society beyond the defence of private property. (Editor)

society and tries to discover its *tendencies*, past and present, its growing needs, intellectual and economical, and in his ideal he merely points out in which direction evolution goes. He distinguishes between the real wants and tendencies of human aggregations and the accidents (want of knowledge, migrations, wars, conquests) which have prevented these tendencies from being satisfied, or temporarily paralysed them. And he concludes that the two most prominent, although often unconscious, tendencies throughout our history have been: a tendency towards integrating labour for the production of all riches in common, so as finally to render it impossible to discriminate the part of the common production due to the separate individual; and a tendency towards the fullest freedom of the individual for the prosecution of all aims beneficial both for himself and for society at large. The ideal of the Anarchist is thus a mere summing-up of what he considers to be the next phase of evolution. It is no longer a matter of faith; it is a matter for scientific discussion.

***

In fact, one of the leading features of our century is the growth of Socialism and the rapid spreading of Socialist views among the working classes. How could it be otherwise? We have witnessed during the last seventy years an unparalleled sudden increase of our powers of production, resulting in an accumulation of wealth which has outstripped the most sanguine expectations. But owing to our wage system, this increase of wealth—due to the combined efforts of men of science, of managers, and workmen as well—has resulted only in an unprevented accumulation of wealth in the hands of the owners of capital; while an increase of misery for great numbers and an insecurity of life for all have been the lot of the workmen. The unskilled labourers, in continuous search for labour, are falling into an unheard of destitution; and even the best paid artisans and the skilled workmen, who undoubtedly are living now a more comfortable life than before, labour under the permanent menace of being thrown, in their turn, into the same conditions as the unskilled paupers, in consequence of some of the continuous and unavoidable fluctuations of industry and caprices of capital. The chasm between the modern millionaire who squanders the produce of human labour in a gorgeous and vain luxury and the pauper reduced to a miserable and insecure existence is thus growing wider and wider, so as to break the very unity of society—the harmony of its life—and to endanger the progress of its further development. At the same time, the working classes are less and less inclined patiently to endure this division of society into two classes, as they themselves become more and more conscious of the wealth-producing power of modern industry, of the part played by labour in the production of wealth and of their own capacities of organisation. In proportion as all classes of the community take a more lively part in public affairs and knowledge spreads among the masses, their longing for equality becomes stronger, and their demands of social reorganisation become louder and louder: they can be ignored no more. The worker claims his share in the riches he produces; he claims his share in the management of production; and he claims not only some additional well-being but also his full rights in the higher enjoyments of science and art. These claims, which formerly were uttered only by the social reformer, begin now to be made by a daily growing minority of those who work in the factory or till the acre; and they so conform with our feelings of justice that they find support in a daily growing minority amidst the privileged classes themselves. Socialism becomes thus *the* idea of the nineteenth century; and neither coercion nor pseudo-reforms can stop its further growth.

Much hope of improvement was placed, of course, in the extension of political rights to the working classes. But these concessions, unsupported as they were by corresponding changes in the economical relations, proved delusory. They did not materially improve the conditions of the great bulk of the workmen. Therefore, the watchword of Socialism is: 'Economical freedom, as the only secure basis for political freedom'. And as long as the present wage system, with all its bad consequences, remains unaltered, the Socialist watchword will continue to inspire the workmen. Socialism will continue to grow until it has realised its programme.

Side by side with this great movement of thought in economical matters, a like movement has been going on with regard to political rights, political organisation and the functions of government. Government has been submitted to the same criticism as capital. While most of the Radicals saw in universal suffrage and republican institutions the last word of political wisdom, a further step was made by the few. The very functions of government and the State, as also their relations to the individual, were submitted to a sharper and deeper criticism. Representative government having been tried by experiment on a wide field, its defects became more and more prominent. It became obvious that these defects are not merely accidental, but inherent in the system itself. Parliament and its executive proved to be unable to attend to all the numberless affairs of the community and to conciliate the varied and often opposite interests of the separate parts of a State. Election proved unable to find out the men who might represent a nation, and manage, otherwise than in a party spirit, the affairs they are compelled to legislate upon. These defects became so striking that the very principles of the representative system were criticised and their justness doubted. Again, the dangers of a centralised government became still more conspicuous when the Socialists came to the front and asked for a further increase of the powers of government by entrusting it with the management of the immense field covered now by the economical relations between individuals. The question was asked whether a government, entrusted with the management of industry and trade would not become a permanent danger for liberty and peace, and whether it even would be able to be a good manager?

The Socialists of the earlier part of this century did not fully realise the immense difficulties of the problem. Convinced as they were of the necessity of economical reforms, most of them took no notice of the need of freedom for the individual; and we have had social reformers ready to submit society to any kind of theocracy, dictatorship or even Caesarism,[3] in order to obtain reforms in a Socialist sense. Therefore, we have seen, in this country and also on the Continent, the division of men of advanced opinions into political Radicals and Socialists—the former looking with distrust on the latter, as they saw in them a danger for the political liberties which have been won by the civilised nations after a long series of struggles. And even now, when the Socialists all over Europe are becoming political parties and profess the democratic faith, there remains among most impartial men a well-founded fear of the *Volksstaat* or 'popular State' being as great a danger for liberty as any form of autocracy, if its government be entrusted with the management of all the social organisation, including the production and distribution of wealth.[4]

---

3   The usurpation of power by a popular dictator or emperor, derived from Julius Caesar (100BCE–44BCE) and his desire to declare himself emperor of Rome. That is, autocratic rule or dictatorship by a charismatic strongman based upon a cult of personality. Napoleon Bonaparte, his nephew Louis Napoleon and Benito Mussolini represented Caesarism. (Editor)

4   A reference to the Marxist notion of a Socialist State, or 'dictatorship of the proletariat', which would nationalise the means of production, defend the revolution and transform society before finally withering away. Marx himself did not use the term, although those close to him did—including the editors of the German Social-Democratic Journal *Volksstaat*, which published his writings—and the concept was used to mean similar things. Anarchists opposed the notion not because they did not think a revolution needed defending but because combining political and economic power in the hands of a hierarchical structure

The evolution of the last forty years has prepared, however, the way for showing the necessity and possibility of a higher form of social organisation which may guarantee economical freedom without reducing the individual to the *rôle* of a slave to the State. The origins of government have been carefully studied, and all metaphysical conceptions as to its divine or 'social contract' derivation having been laid aside, it appears that it is among us of a relatively modern origin, and that its powers have grown precisely in proportion as the division of society into the privileged and unprivileged classes was growing in the course of ages. Representative government has also been reduced to its real value—that of an instrument which has rendered services in the struggle against autocracy, but not an ideal of free political organisation. As to the system of philosophy which saw in the State (the *Kulturstaat*) a leader of progress, it was more and more shaken as it became evident that progress is the more effective when it is not checked by State interference.[5] It has thus become obvious that a further advance in social life does not lie in the direction of a further concentration of power and regulative functions in the hands of a governing body but in the direction of decentralisation, both territorial and functional—in a subdivision of public functions with respect both to their sphere of action and to the character of the functions; it is in the abandonment to the initiative of freely constituted groups of all those functions which are now considered as the functions of government.

This current of thought has found its expression not merely in literature, but also, to a limited extent, in life. The uprise of the Paris Commune, followed by that of the Commune of Cartagena—a movement of which the historical bearing seems to have been quite overlooked in this country—opened

---

like a State would produce a dictatorship *over* the proletariat. The fate of every Marxist revolution has confirmed this analysis. (Editor)

5   The *Kulturstaat* was a notion of Idealist philosophers, especially Hegel, by which an all-powerful State represents the whole nation. (Editor)

a new page of history.[6] If we analyse not only this movement in itself, but also the impression it left in the minds and the tendencies manifested during the communal revolution, we must recognise in it an indication showing that, in the future, human agglomerations which are more advanced in their social development will try to start an independent life; and that they will endeavour to convert the more backward parts of a nation by example, instead of imposing their opinions by law and force or submitting themselves to the majority rule, which always is a mediocrity rule. At the same time the failure of representative government within the Commune itself proved that self-government and self-administration must be carried further than in a merely territorial sense; to be effective they must also be carried into the various functions of life within the free community; a merely territorial limitation of the sphere of action of government will not do—representative government being as deficient in a city as it is in a nation. Life gave thus a further point in favour of the no-government theory, and a new impulse to anarchist thought.

***

Anarchists recognise the justice of both the just-mentioned tendencies towards economical and political freedom, and see in them two different manifestations of the very same need of equality which constitutes the very essence of all struggles mentioned by history. Therefore, in common with all Socialists, the Anarchist says to the political reformer: 'No substantial reform in the sense of political equality and no limitation of the powers of government can be made as long as society is divided into two hostile camps, and the labourer remains, economically

---

6   A reference to a series of communal revolts which swept France and Spain between 1870 and 1873, the most famous being the Paris Commune of 1871. These, and the lessons gained from them, were a central aspect of Kropotkin's politics. (Editor)

speaking, a serf to his employer'. But to the Popular State Socialist we say also: 'You cannot modify the existing conditions of property without deeply modifying at the same time the political organisation. You must limit the powers of government and renounce Parliamentary rule. To each new economical phase of life corresponds a new political phase. Absolute monarchy—that is, Court rule—corresponded to the system of serfdom. Representative government corresponds to capital rule. Both, however, are class rule. But in a society where the distinction between capitalist and labourer has disappeared, there is no need of such a government; it would be an anachronism, a nuisance. Free workers would require a free organisation, and this cannot have another basis than free agreement and free co-operation, without sacrificing the autonomy of the individual to the all-pervading interference of the State. The no-capitalist system implies the no-government system'.

Meaning thus the emancipation of man from the oppressive powers of capitalist and government, as well, the system of Anarchy becomes a synthesis of the two powerful currents of thought which characterise our century.

***

In arriving at these conclusions, Anarchy proves to be in accordance with the conclusions arrived at by the philosophy of evolution. By bringing to light the plasticity of organisation, the philosophy of evolution has shown the admirable adaptivity of organisms to their conditions of life, and the ensuing development of such faculties as render more complete both the adaptations of the aggregates to their surroundings and those of each of the constituent parts of the aggregate to the needs of free co-operation. It has familiarised us with the circumstance that throughout organic nature the capacities for life in common grow in proportion as the integration of organisms into compound aggregates becomes more and more complete;

and it has enforced thus the opinion already expressed by social moralists as to the perfectibility of human nature. It has shown us that, in the long run of the struggle for existence, 'the fittest' will prove to be those who combine intellectual knowledge with the knowledge necessary for the production of wealth, and not those who are now the richest because they, or their ancestors, have been momentarily the strongest. By showing that the 'struggle for existence' must be conceived not merely in its restricted sense of a struggle between individuals for the means of subsistence but in its wider sense of adaptation of all individuals of the species to the best conditions for the survival of the species, as well as for the greatest possible sum of life and happiness for each and all, it has permitted us to deduce the laws of moral science from the social needs and habits of mankind. It has showed us the infinitesimal part played by the natural growth of altruistic feelings, which develop as soon as the conditions of life favour their growth. It thus enforced the opinion of social reformers as to the necessity of modifying the conditions of life for improving man, instead of trying to improve human nature by moral teachings while life works in an opposite direction. Finally, by studying human society from the biological point of view, it has come to the conclusions arrived at by Anarchists from the study of history and present tendencies as to further progress being in the line of socialisation of wealth and integrated labour, combined with the fullest possible freedom of the individual.

It is not a mere coincidence that Herbert Spencer, whom we may consider as a pretty fair expounder of the philosophy of evolution, has been brought to conclude, with regard to political organisation, that 'that form of society towards which we are progressing' is 'one in which *government* will be reduced to the smallest amount possible, and *freedom* increased to the greatest amount possible'.[7] When he opposes in these

---

7   *Essays*, vol. iii. I am fully aware that in the very same *Essays*, a few
     pages further, Herbert Spencer destroys the force of the foregoing

words the conclusions of his synthetic philosophy to those of Auguste Comte, he arrives at very nearly the same conclusion as Proudhon[8] and Bakunin.[9] More than that, the very methods of argumentation and the illustrations resorted to by Herbert Spencer (daily supply of food, post office and so on) are the same which we find in the writings of the Anarchists. The channels of thought were the same, although both were unaware of each other's endeavours.

Again, when Mr. Spencer so powerfully, and even not without a touch of passion, argues (in his Appendix to the third edition of the *Data of Ethics*) that human societies are marching towards a state when a further identification of altruism with egoism will be made 'in the sense that personal gratification will come from the gratification of others'; when he says that 'we are shown, undeniably, that it is a perfectly possible thing for organisms to become so adjusted to the requirements of their lives, that energy expended for the general welfare may not only be adequate to check energy expended for the individual welfare, but may come to subordinate it so far as to leave individual welfare no greater part than is necessary for

---

statement by the following words: 'Not only do I contend', he says, 'that the restraining power of the State over individuals and bodies, or classes of individuals, is requisite, but I have contended that it should be exercised much more effectually and carried much farther than at present' (p. 145). And although he tries to establish a distinction between the (desirable) negatively regulative functions of government, we know that no such distinction can be established in political life, and that the former necessarily lead to, and even imply, the latter. But we must distinguish between the system of philosophy and its interpreter. All we can say is that Herbert Spencer does not endorse all the conclusions which ought to be drawn from his system of philosophy.

8   *Idee generale sur la Revolution au XIX siecle*; and *Confessions d'un revolutionnaire*. [Extracts from both books are included in *Property Is Theft!*—Editor]

9   *Lettres a un Francais sur la crise aetuelle*; *L'Empire knouto-germanique*; *The State's Idea and Anarchy* (Russian). [Extracts from these works are included in *Bakunin on Anarchism* (Montréal: Black Rose Books, 1980)—Editor]

maintenance of individual life'—provided the conditions for such relations between the individual and the community be maintained[10]—he derives from the study of nature the very same conclusions as the forerunners of Anarchy, Fourier and Robert Owen, derived from a study of human character.

When we see further Mr. Bain so forcibly elaborating the theory of moral habits, and the French philosopher M. Guyau unveiling in a most remarkable work the basis of *Morality without Obligation or Sanction*;[11] when J.S. Mill so sharply criticises representative government and discusses the problem of liberty, although failing to establish its necessary conditions;[12] when modern biology brings us to understand the importance of free co-operation and mutual aid in the animal world; when Lewis Morgan (in *Ancient Society*) shows us the parasitical development of State and property amidst the free institutions of our earliest ancestors, and modern history follows the same lines of argumentation—when, in short, every year, by bringing some new arguments to the philosophy of evolution, adds at the same time some new arguments to the philosophy of Anarchy—we must recognise that this last, although differing

---

10 Pages 300 to 302. In fact, the whole of this chapter, which did not appear in the first two editions, ought to be quoted.

11 Alexander Bain (1818–1903) was a Scottish philosopher and psychologist; Jean-Marie Guyau (1854–1888), French philosopher and poet whose 1884 work *Esquisse d'une morale sans obligation ni sanction* (*A Sketch of Morality Independent of Obligation or Sanction* [London: Watts, 1898]) deeply impressed Kropotkin. Kropotkin later discussed his ideas in Chapter XIII of the posthumously published *Ethics: Origin and Development* and called him 'an anarchist without knowing it' in the 1889 pamphlet *Anarchist Morality*. (Editor)

12 John Stuart Mill (1806–1878), English economist and philosopher. Kropotkin is referring to his books *On Liberty* (1859) and *Considerations on Representative Government* (1861). Always somewhat critical of the reality of capitalism, towards the end of his life Mill came to advocate what would now be called market socialism—that is, an economic system based on workers' co-operatives selling the product of their labour on the market. This had distinct similarities with Proudhon's mutualism. (Editor)

as to its starting points, follows the same sound methods of scientific investigation.[13] Our confidence in its conclusions is still more increased. The difference between Anarchists and the just-named philosophers may be immense as to the presumed speed of evolution and as to the line of conduct which one ought to assume as soon as he has had an insight into the aims towards which society is marching. No attempt, however, has been made scientifically to determine the ratio of evolution, nor has the chief element of the problem (the state of mind of the masses) ever been taken into account by the evolutionist philosophers. As to bringing one's action into accordance with his philosophical conceptions, we know that, unhappily, intellect and will are too often separated by a chasm not to be filled by mere philosophical speculations, however deep and elaborate.

***

There is, however, between the just-named philosophers and the Anarchists a wide difference on one point of primordial importance. This difference is the stranger as it arises on a point which might be discussed figures in hand, and which constitutes the very basis of all further deductions, as it belongs to what biological sociology would describe as the physiology of nutrition.

There is, in fact, a widely spread fallacy, maintained by Mr. Spencer and many others, as to the causes of the misery which we see round about us. It was affirmed forty years ago, and it is affirmed now by Mr. Spencer and his followers, that misery in civilised society is due to our insufficient production, or rather to the circumstance that 'population presses upon the means

---

13 Lewis Henry Morgan (1818–1881) was a pioneering American anthropologist and social theorist, cited by many scholars including Charles Darwin and Frederick Engels. In *Ancient Society* (1877) he developed a theory of social evolution based on three stages of human progress, from Savagery through Barbarism to Civilisation. (Editor)

of subsistence'. It would be of no use to inquire into the origin of such a misrepresentation of facts, which might be easily verified. It may have its origin in inherited misconceptions which have nothing to do with the philosophy of evolution. But to be maintained and advocated by philosophers, there must be, in the conceptions of these philosophers, some confusion as to the different aspects of the struggle for existence. Sufficient importance is not given to the difference between the struggle which goes on among organisms which do *not* co-operate for providing the means of subsistence and those which *do* so. In this last case, again there must be some confusion between those aggregates whose members find their means of subsistence in the ready-made produce of the vegetable and animal kingdom and those whose members artificially grow their means of subsistence and are enabled to increase (to a yet unknown amount) the productivity of each spot of the surface of the globe. Hunters who hunt, each of them for his own sake, and hunters who unite into societies for hunting stand quite differently with regard to the means of subsistence. But the difference is still greater between the hunters who take their means of subsistence as they are in nature and to civilised men who grow their food and produce by machinery all requisites for a comfortable life. In this last case—the stock of potential energy in nature being little short of infinite in comparison with the present population of the globe—the means of availing ourselves of the stock of energy are increased and perfected precisely in proportion to the density of population and to the previously accumulated stock of technical knowledge; so that for human beings who are in possession of scientific knowledge, and co-operate for the artificial production of the means of subsistence and comfort, the law is quite the reverse of that of Malthus.[14] The accumulation of means of subsistence and

---

14 A reference to Thomas Robert Malthus (1766–1834) and his so-called law of population, which blamed the poverty of his time on the tendency of population (that is to say, numbers of working-class people)

comfort is going on at a much speedier rate than the increase of population. The only conclusion which we can deduce from the laws of evolution and of multiplication of effects is that the available amount of means of subsistence increases at a rate which increases itself in proportion as population becomes denser—unless it be artificially (and temporarily) checked by some defects of social organisation. As to our *powers* of production (our potential production), they increase at a still speedier rate in proportion as scientific knowledge grows, the means for spreading it are rendered easier and inventive genius is stimulated by all previous inventions.

If the fallacy as to the pressure of population on the means of subsistence could be maintained a hundred years ago, it can be maintained no more, since we have witnessed the effects of science on industry, and the enormous increase of our productive powers during the last hundred years. We know, in fact, that while the growth of population of England has been from 16½ millions in 1844 to 26¾ millions in 1883, showing thus an increase of 62 per cent, the growth of national wealth (as testified by schedule A of the Income Tax Act) has increased twice as fast; it has grown from 221 for 507½ millions—that is, by 130 per cent. And we know that the same increase of wealth has taken place in France, where population remains almost stationary, and that it has gone on at a still speedier rate in the United States, where population is increasing every year by immigration.

---

to exceed food supplies rather than an unjust economic system, as the radicals he attacked (like William Godwin) were arguing. His assertions were well received—for obvious reasons—by the ruling class of his and subsequent times, while radicals and Socialists viewed them as apologetics Proudhon, for example, wrote against Malthus on many occasions, most famously in his article 'The Malthusians'—included in *Property is Theft!: A Pierre-Joseph Proudhon Anthology* (Edinburgh: AK Press, 2011). It must be stressed that Kropotkin's critique has turned out to be correct. (Editor)

But the figures just mentioned, while showing the real increase of production, give only a faint idea of what our production might be under a more reasonable economical organisation. We know well that the owners of capital, while trying to produce more wares with fewer 'hands', are continually endeavouring to limit the production, in order to sell at higher prices. When the profits of a concern are going down, the owner of the capital limits the production, or totally suspends it, and prefers to engage his capital in foreign loans or shares in Patagonian gold mines. Just now there are plenty of pitmen in England who ask for nothing better than to be permitted to extract coal and supply with cheap fuel the households where children are shivering before empty chimneys. There are thousands of weavers who ask for nothing better than to weave stuffs in order to replace the ragged dress of the poor with decent clothing. And so in all branches of industry. How can we talk about a want of means of subsistence when thousands of factories lie idle in Great Britain alone; and when there are, just now, thousands and thousands of unemployed in London alone; thousands of men who would consider themselves happy if they were permitted to transform (under the guidance of experienced men) the clay of Middlesex into a rich soil and to cover with cornfields and orchards the acres of meadowland which now yield only a few pounds' worth of hay? But they are prevented from doing so by the owners of the land, of the weaving factory and of the coal mine, because capital finds it more advantageous to supply the Khedive[15] with harems and the Russian government with 'strategic railways' and Krupp guns. Of course, the maintenance of harems *pays*: it gives 10 or 15 per cent on the capital, while the extraction of coal does not pay—that is, it brings 3 or 5 per cent—and that is a sufficient reason for limiting the production and permitting would-be

---

15   *Khedive* was the title of the Turkish viceroy of Egypt from 1867 to 1914, a byword for luxury and corruption. (Editor)

economists to indulge in reproaches to the working classes as to their too rapid multiplication!

***

Here we have instances of a direct and conscious limitation of production, due to the circumstance that the requisites for production belong to the few, and that these few have the right of disposing of them at their will, without caring about the interests of the community. But there is also the indirect and unconscious limitation of production—that which results from squandering the produce of human labour in luxury, instead of applying it to a further increase of production.

This last cannot even be estimated in figures, but a walk through the rich shops of any city and a glance at the manner in which money is squandered now, can give an approximate idea of this indirect limitation. When a rich man spends a thousand pounds for his stables, he squanders five to six thousand days of human labour, which might be used, under a better social organisation, for supplying with comfortable homes those who are compelled to live now in dens. And when a lady spends a hundred pounds for her dress, we cannot but say that she squanders, at least, two years of human labour, which, again under a better organisation, might have supplied a hundred women with decent dresses, and much more if applied to a further improvement of the instruments of production. Preachers thunder against luxury, because it is shameful to squander money for feeding and sheltering hounds and horses, when thousands live in the East End on sixpence a day and other thousands have not even their miserable sixpence every day. But the economist sees more than that in our modern luxury: when millions of days of labour are spent every year for the satisfaction of the stupid vanity of the rich, he says that so many millions of workers have been diverted from the manufacture of those useful instruments which would permit us to decuple and centuple our present production of means of subsistence and of requisites for comfort.

In short, if we take into account both the real and the potential increase of our wealth and consider both the direct and indirect limitation of production, which are unavoidable under our present economical system, we must recognise that the supposed 'pressure of population on the means of subsistence' is a mere fallacy, repeated, like many other fallacies, without even taking the trouble of submitting it to a moment's criticism. The causes of the present social disease must be sought elsewhere.

***

Let us take a civilised country. The forests have been cleared, the swamps drained. Thousands of roads and railways intersect it in all directions; the rivers have been rendered navigable and the seaports are of easy access. Canals connect the seas. The rocks have been pierced by deep shafts; thousands of manufactures cover the land. Science has taught man how to use the energy of nature for the satisfaction of his needs. Cities have slowly grown in the course of ages, and treasures of science and art are accumulated in these centres of civilisation. But—who has made all these marvels?

The combined efforts of scores of generations have contributed towards the achievement of these results. The forests have been cleared centuries ago; millions of men have spent years and years of labour in draining the swamps, in tracing the roads, in building the railways. Other millions have built the cities and created the civilisation we boast of. Thousands of inventors, mostly unknown, mostly dying in poverty and neglect, have elaborated the machinery in which man admires his genius. Thousands of writers, philosophers and men of science, supported by many thousands of compositors, printers and other labourers whose name is legion, have contributed to elaborating and spreading knowledge, to dissipating errors, to creating the atmosphere of scientific thought, without which the marvels of our century never would have been brought to life. The genius of a Mayer and a Grove, the patient work of a Joule, surely have done more to give a new start to modern industry than all the capitalists of the world;[16] but these men of genius themselves are, in their turn, the children of industry: thousands of engines had to transform heat into mechanical force and mechanical force into sound, light and electricity— and they had to do so for years, every day, under the eyes of humanity—before some of our contemporaries proclaimed the mechanical origin of heat and the correlation of physical forces, and before we ourselves became prepared to listen to them and understand their teachings. Who knows for how many decades we should continue to be ignorant of this theory which now revolutionises industry were it not for the inventive powers and skill of those unknown workers who have improved the steam engine, who have brought all its parts to perfection so as to make steam more manageable than a horse and to render the use of the engine nearly universal? But the same is true with regard to each smallest part of our machinery. In each machine, however simple, we may read a whole history—a long history of sleepless nights, of delusions and joys, of partial inventions and partial improvements which have brought it to its present state. Nay, nearly every new machine is a synthesis, a result of thousands of partial inventions made not only in one special department of machinery but in all departments of the wide field of mechanics.

Our cities, connected by roads and brought into easy communication with all peopled parts of the globe, are the growth of centuries; and each house in these cities, each factory, each shop, derives its value, its very *raison d'etre*, from the fact that it is situated on a spot of the globe where thousands or millions

16   Three well-known physicists: Julius Robert Mayer (1814–1878), William Robert Grove (1811–1896) and James Prescott Joule (1818–1889). (Editor)

have gathered together. Every smallest part of the immense whole which we call the wealth of civilised nations derives its value precisely from being a part of this whole. What would be the value of an immense London shop or warehouse were it not situated precisely in London, which has become the gathering spot for five millions of human beings? And what the value of our coal pits, our manufactures, our shipbuilding yards, were it not for the immense traffic which goes on across the seas, for the railways which transport mountains of merchandise, for the cities which number their inhabitants by millions? Who is, then, the individual who has the right to step forward and, laying his hands on the smallest part of this immense whole, to say, '*I* have produced this; it belongs to *me*'? And how can we discriminate, in this immense interwoven whole, the part which the isolated individual may appropriate to himself with the slightest approach to justice? Houses and streets, canals and railways, machines and works of art, all these have been created by the combined efforts of generations past and present, of men living on these islands and men living thousands of miles away.

***

But it has happened in the long run of ages that everything which permits men further to increase their production, or even to continue it, has been appropriated by the few. The land, which derives its value precisely from its being necessary for an ever-increasing population, belongs to the few, who may prevent the community from cultivating it. The coal pits, which represent the labour of generations, and which also derive their value from the wants of the manufactures and railroads, from the immense trade carried on and the density of population (what is the value of coal layers in Transbaikalia?), belong again to the few, who have even the right of stopping the extraction of coal if they choose to give another use to their capital. The lace-weaving machine, which represents, in its present state of perfection, the work of three generations of Lancashire weavers, belongs again to the few; and if the grandsons of the very same weaver who invented the first lace-weaving machine claim their rights of bringing one of these machines into motion, they will be told 'Hands off! this machine does not belong to you!' The railroads, which mostly would be useless heaps of iron if Great Britain had not its present dense population, its industry, trade, and traffic, belong again to the few—to a few shareholders, who may even not know where the railway is situated which brings them a yearly income larger than that of a medieval king; and if the children of those people who died by thousands in digging the tunnels would gather and go—a ragged and starving crowd— to ask bread or work from the shareholders, they would be met with bayonets and bullets.

Who is the sophist who will dare to say that such an organisation is just? But what is unjust cannot be beneficial to mankind; and *it is not*. In consequence of this monstrous organisation, the son of a workman, when he is able to work, finds no acre to till, no machine to set in motion, unless he agrees to sell his labour for a sum inferior to its real value. His father and grandfather have contributed to drain the field or erect the factory to the full extent of their capacities—and nobody can do more than that—but he comes into the world more destitute than a savage. If he resorts to agriculture, he will be permitted to cultivate a plot of land, but on the condition that he gives up one quarter of his crop to the landlord. If he resorts to industry, he will be permitted to work, but on the condition that out of the thirty shillings he has produced, ten shillings or more will be pocketed by the owner of the machine. We cry against the feudal baron who did not permit anyone to settle on the land otherwise than on payment of one quarter of the crops to the lord of the manor; but we continue to do as they did—we extend their system. The forms have changed, but the essence has remained the same. And the workman is compelled to accept the feudal conditions which we call 'free contrast', because nowhere will he find better conditions. Everything has been appropriated by somebody; he *must* accept the bargain, or starve.

***

Owing to this circumstance our production takes a wrong turn. It takes no care of the needs of the community; its only aim is to increase the profits of the capitalist. Therefore—the continuous fluctuations of industry, the crises coming periodically nearly every ten years, and throwing out of employment several hundred thousand men who are brought to complete misery, whose children grow up in the gutter, ready to become inmates of the prison and workhouse. The workmen being unable to purchase with their wages the riches they are producing, industry must search for markets elsewhere, amidst the middle classes of other nations. It must find markets, in the East, in Africa, anywhere; it must increase, by trade, the number of its serfs in Egypt, in India, on the Congo. But everywhere it finds competitors in other nations which rapidly enter into the same line of industrial development. And wars, continuous wars, must be fought for the supremacy on the world market—wars for the possession of the East, wars for getting possession of the seas, wars for having the right of imposing heavy duties on foreign merchandise. The thunder of European guns never ceases; whole generations are slaughtered from time to time; and we spend in armaments the third of the revenue of our States—a revenue raised, the poor know with what difficulties. Education is the privilege of the few. Not because we can find no teachers, not because the workman's son and daughter are less able to receive instruction, but because one can receive no reasonable instruction when at the age of fifteen he descends into the mine or goes selling newspapers in the streets. Society becomes divided into two hostile camps; and no freedom is possible under such conditions. While the Radical asks for a further extension of liberty, the statesman answers him that a further increase of liberty would bring about an uprising of the paupers; and those political liberties which have cost so dear are replaced by coercion, by exceptional laws, by military rule. And finally, the injustice of our partition of wealth exercises the most deplorable effect on our morality. Our principles of morality say: 'Love your neighbour as yourself'; but let a child follow this principle and take off his coat to give it to the shivering pauper, and his mother will tell him that he must understand moral principles in their right sense. If he lives according to them, he will go barefoot, without alleviating the misery round about him! Morality is good on the lips, not in deeds. Our preachers say, 'Who works, prays', and everybody endeavours to make others work for himself. They say, 'Never lie!' and politics is a big lie. And we accustom ourselves and our children to live under this double-faced morality, which is hypocrisy, and to conciliate our double-facedness by sophistry. Hypocrisy and sophistry become the very basis of our life. But society cannot live under such a morality. It cannot last so: it must, it will, be changed.

The question is thus no more a mere question of bread. It covers the whole field of human activity. But it has at its bottom a question of social economy, and we conclude: the means of production and of satisfaction of all needs of society, having been created by the common efforts of all, must be at the disposal of all. The private appropriation of requisites for production is neither just nor beneficial. All must be placed on the same footing as producers and consumers of wealth. That will be the only way for society to step out of the bad conditions which have been created by centuries of wars and oppression. That will be the only guarantee for further progress in a direction of equality and freedom, which have always been the real, although unspoken, goal of humanity.

II

The views taken in the above as to the combination of efforts being the chief source of our wealth explain why more Anarchists see in Communism the only equitable solution as to the adequate remuneration of individual efforts. There was a time when a family engaged in agriculture and supplemented by a few domestic trades could consider the corn they raised and the plain woollen cloth they wove as production of their own and nobody else's labour. Even then such a view was not quite correct: there were forests cleared and roads built by common efforts; and even then the family had continually to apply for communal help, as it is still the case in so many village communities. But now, under the extremely interwoven state of industry, of which each branch supports all others, such an individualistic view can be held no more. If the iron trade and the cotton industry of this country have reached so high a degree of development, they have done so owing to the parallel growth of thousands of other industries, great and small; to the extension of the railway system; to an increase of knowledge among both the skilled engineers and the mass of the workmen; to a certain training in organisation slowly developed among British producers; and, above all, to the world trade which has itself grown up, thanks to works executed thousands of miles away. The Italians who died from cholera in digging the Suez Canal, or from 'tunnel disease' in the St. Gothard Tunnel, have contributed as much towards the enrichment of this country as the British girl who is prematurely growing old in serving a machine at Manchester; and this girl is much as the engineer who made a labour saving improvement in our machinery. How can we pretend to estimate the exact part of each of them in the riches accumulated around us?

We may admire the inventive genius or the organising capacities of an iron lord; but we must recognise that all his genius and energy would not realise one-tenth of what they realise here if they were spent dealing with Mongolian shepherds or Siberian peasants instead of British workmen, British engineers and trustworthy managers. An English millionaire who succeeded in giving a powerful impulse to a branch of home industry was asked the other day what were, in his opinion, the real causes of his success? His answer was: 'I always sought out the right man for a given branch of the concern, and I left him full independence—maintaining, of course, for myself the general supervision'. 'Did you never fail to find such men?' was the next question. 'Never'. 'But in the new branches which you introduced you wanted a number of new inventions'. 'No doubt; we spend thousands in buying patents'. This little colloquy sums up, in my opinion, the real case of those industrial undertakings which are quoted by the advocates of 'an adequate remuneration of individual efforts' in the shape of millions bestowed on the managers of prosperous industries. It shows in how far the efforts are really 'individual'. Leaving aside the thousand conditions which sometimes permit a man to show, and sometimes prevent him from showing, his capacities to their full extent, it might be asked in how far the same capacities could bring out the same results, if the very same employer could find no trustworthy managers and no skilled workmen, and if hundreds of inventions were not stimulated by the mechanical turn of mind of so many inhabitants of this country. British industry is the work of the British nation—nay, of Europe and India taken together—not of separate individuals.

***

While holding this synthetic view on production, the Anarchists cannot consider, like the Collectivists, that a remuneration which would be proportionate to the hours of labour spent by each person in the production of riches may be an ideal, or even an approach to an ideal, society.[17] Without entering here into a discussion as to how far the exchange value of each merchandise is really measured now by the amount of labour necessary for its production—a separate study must be devoted to the subject—we must say that the Collectivist ideal seems to us merely unrealisable in a society which would be brought to consider the necessaries for production as a common property. Such a society would be compelled to abandon the wage system altogether. It appears impossible that the mitigated Individualism of the Collectivist school could co-exist with the partial Communism implied by holding land and machinery in common—unless imposed by a powerful government, much more powerful than all those of our own times. The present wage system has grown up from the appropriation of the necessities for production by the few; it was a necessary condition for the growth of the present capitalist production; and it cannot outlive it, even if an attempt be made to pay to the worker the full value of his produce, and hours-of-labour-cheques be substituted for money. Common possession of the necessaries for production implies that common enjoyment of the fruits of the common production; and we consider that an equitable organisation of society can only arise when every wage system is abandoned, and when everybody, contributing for the common well-being to the full extent of his capacities, shall enjoy also from the common stock of society to the fullest possible extent of his needs.

***

---

17 By Collectivists, Kropotkin is primarily referring to the mainstream of the socialist movement, namely the Social-Democratic parties, rather than anarchists who called themselves by that name in the 1860s and 1870s. While his critique is certainly pertinent to those libertarians, with the possible exception of Spain most anarchists by this time had accepted libertarian communism as their ideal. (Editor)

We maintain, moreover, not only that Communism is a desirable state of society, but that the growing tendency of modern society is precisely towards Communism—free Communism— notwithstanding the seemingly contradictory growth of individualism. In the growth of individualism (especially during the last three centuries) we merely see the endeavours of the individual towards emancipating himself from the steadily growing powers of capital and the State. But side by side with this growth we see also, throughout history up to our own times, the latent struggle of the producers of wealth to maintain the partial Communism of old, as well as to reintroduce Communist principles in a new shape, as soon as favourable conditions permit it. As soon as the communes of the tenth, eleventh, and twelfth centuries were enabled to start their own independent life, they gave a wide extension to work in common, to trade in common, and to a partial consumption in common. All this has disappeared; but the rural commune fights a hard struggle to maintain its old features, and it succeeds in maintaining them in many places of Eastern Europe, Switzerland, and even France and Germany; while new organisations based on the same principles never fail to grow up wherever it is possible. Notwithstanding the egotistic turn given to the public mind by the merchant production of our century, the Communist tendency is continually reasserting itself and trying to make its way into the public life. The penny bridge disappears before the public bridge; and the turnpike road disappears before the free road. The same spirit pervades thousands of other institutions. Museums, free libraries and free public schools; parks and pleasure grounds; paved and lighted streets, free for everybody's use; water supplied to private dwellings, with a growing tendency towards disregarding the exact amount of it used by the individual; tramways and railways which have already begun to introduce the season ticket or the uniform tax and will surely go much further on this line when they are no longer private property: all these are tokens showing in which direction further progress is to be expected.

It is in the direction of putting the wants of the individual *above* the valuation of the services he has rendered, or might render, to society; in considering society as a whole, so intimately connected together that a service rendered to any individual is a service rendered to the whole society. The librarian of the British Museum does not ask the reader what have been his previous services to society, he simply gives him the book he requires; and for a uniform fee, a scientific society leaves its gardens and museums at the free disposal of each member. The crew of a lifeboat do not ask whether the men of a distressed ship are entitled to be rescued at a risk of life; and the Prisoners' Aid Society do not inquire what the released prisoner is worth. Here are men in need of a service; they are *fellow* men, and no further rights are required. And if this very city, so egotistic today, be visited by a public calamity—let it be besieged, for example, like Paris in 1871, and experience during the siege a want of food—this very same city would be unanimous in proclaiming that the first needs to be satisfied are those of the children and old, no matter what services they may render or have rendered to society. And it would take care of the active defenders of the city, whatever the degrees of gallantry displayed by each of them. But this tendency already existing, nobody will deny, I suppose, that in proportion as humanity is relieved from its hard struggle for life the same tendency will grow stronger. If our productive powers be fully applied to increasing the stock of the staple necessities for life; if a modification of the present conditions of property increased the number of producers by all those who are not producers of wealth now; and if manual labour reconquered its place of honour in society—all this decuplating our production and rendering labour easier and more attractive—the Communist tendencies already existing would immediately enlarge their sphere of application.

***

Taking all this into account, and still more the practical aspects of the question as to how private property *might* become common property, most of the Anarchists maintain that the very next step to be made by society, as soon as the present *régime* of property undergoes a modification, will be in a Communist sense. We are Communists. But our Communism is not that of either the Phalanstery[18] or the authoritarian school: it is Anarchist Communism, Communism without government, free Communism. It is a synthesis of the two chief aims prosecuted by humanity since the dawn of its history—economical freedom and political freedom.

I have already said that means no-government. We know well that the word 'anarchy' is also used in current phraseology as synonymous with disorder. But that meaning of 'anarchy', being a derived one, implies at least two suppositions. It implies, first, that whenever there is no government there is disorder; and it implies, moreover, that order, due to a strong government and a strong police, is always beneficial. Both implications, however, are anything but proved. There is plenty of order—we should say, of harmony—in many branches of human activity where the government, happily, does not interfere. As to the beneficial effects of order, the kind of order that reigned at Naples under the Bourbons surely was not preferable to some disorder started by Garibaldi;[19] while

---

18 A phalanstery (*phalanstère*) was a self-contained structure which housed a co-operative community advocated by Charles Fourier in the early 1800s. It was envisioned as a highly organised and highly regulated community living under one roof and working together for mutual benefit. A member's quality of life would vary with their work, 'talent' and 'capital' (amount invested). Everyone would work while a spirit of competition would exist in the shape of emulation. (Editor)

19 Giuseppe Garibaldi (1807–1882) was an Italian general, politician and nationalist. He personally commanded and fought in many military campaigns that led eventually to Italian unification. His volunteer troops fought in many wars for Italian unification, most famously the *Expedition of the Thousand* in support of popular uprisings in Messina and Palermo in 1860, which led to the overthrow of the Bourbon

the Protestants of this country will probably say that the good deal of disorder made by Luther was preferable, at any rate, to the order which reigned under the Pope.[20] As to the proverbial 'order' which was once 'restored at Warsaw', there are, I suppose, no two opinions about it.[21] While all agree that harmony is always desirable, there is no such unanimity about order, and still less about the 'order' which is supposed to reign in our modern societies; so that we have no objection whatever to the use of the word 'anarchy' as a negation of what has been often described as order.[22]

***

By taking for our watchword anarchy, in its sense of no-government, we intend to express a pronounced tendency of human society. In history we see that precisely those epochs when small parts of humanity broke down the power of their

---

autocratic dynasty which ruled Southern Italy, eventually leading to the unification of Italy under a constitutional monarchy. (Editor)

20 A reference to the Protestant Reformation, started by Martin Luther (1483–1546) in 1517. (Editor)

21 A reference to the January Uprising of 1863 against the occupation of Poland by the Russian Empire. The revolt was put down by the Russia Governor General Count Mikhail Nikolayevich Muravyov (1796–1866), with thousands killed in battle and, afterwards, 128 hanged and around ten thousand men and women exiled to Siberia. Muravyov proclaimed: 'Order has been restored in Warsaw'. (Editor)

22 This reflects an earlier discussion—included as a chapter of *Words of a Rebel* entitled 'Order'—where Kropotkin contrasts the 'disorder' of the struggle for freedom by the many and the 'order' of oppression and exploitation by the few. It must be noted that the examples given reflect Kropotkin tailoring his arguments to his audience, knowing that all these examples of rebellion would be viewed sympathetically by the readership of the *Nineteenth Century* magazine where this work first appeared. He obviously hoped to show the readership the contradiction between supporting rebels against political and religious autocracy and opposing working-class rebels against economic autocracy. (Editor)

rulers and reassumed their freedom were epochs of the greatest progress, economical and intellectual. Be it the growth of
the free cities, whose unrivalled monuments—free work of
free associations of workers—still testify of the revival of mind
and of the well-being of the citizen; be it the great movement
which gave birth to the Reformation—those epochs when the
individual recovered some part of his freedom witnessed the
greatest progress. And if we carefully watch the present development of civilised nations, we cannot fail to discover in it a
marked and ever-growing movement towards limiting more
and more the sphere of action of government, so as to leave
more and more liberty to the initiative of the individual. After
having tried all kinds of government and endeavouring to
solve the insoluble problem of having a government 'which
might compel the individual to obedience, without escaping
itself from obedience to collectivity', humanity is trying now
to free itself from the bonds of any government whatever and
to respond to its needs of organisation by the free understanding between individuals prosecuting the same common aims.
Home Rule, even for the smallest territorial unit or group,
becomes a growing need;[23] free agreement is becoming a substitute for the law; and free co-operation a substitute for governmental guardianship. One after the other those functions
which were considered as the functions of government during
the last two centuries are disputed; society moves better the
less it is governed. And the more we study the advance made
in this direction, as well as the inadequacy of governments to
fulfil the expectations placed in them, the more we are bound

---

23 For Kropotkin's contemporary British readers, Irish Home Rule was
    the dominant political question of British and Irish politics at the end
    of the nineteenth century (the first Irish Home Rule Bill was defeated
    in the House of Commons in 1886). This is one of many examples
    in the essay in which we see Kropotkin tailoring his arguments and
    terminology to his audience, given that Home Rule for Ireland was a
    popular cause in the British liberal circles which read the journal in
    which this work first appeared. (Editor)

to conclude that humanity, by steadily limiting the functions of government, is marching towards reducing them finally to *nil*; and we already foresee a state of society where the liberty of the individual will be limited by no laws, no bonds—by nothing else but his own social habits and the necessity which everyone feels of finding co-operation, support and sympathy among his neighbours.

Of course, the no-government ethics will meet with at least as many objections as the no-capital economics. Our minds have been so nurtured in prejudices as to the providential functions of government that Anarchist ideas *must* be received with distrust. Our whole education, from childhood to the grave, nurtures the belief in the necessity of a government and its beneficial effects. Systems of philosophy have been elaborated to support this view; history has been written from this standpoint; theories of law have been circulated and taught for the same purpose. All politics are based on the same principles, each politician saying to the people he wants to support him: 'Give me the governmental power; I will, I can, relieve you from the hardships of your present life'. All our education is permeated with the same teachings. We may open any book of sociology, history, law or ethics: everywhere we find government, its organisation, its deeds, playing so prominent a part that we grow accustomed to suppose that the State and the political men are everything; that there is nothing behind the big statesmen. The same teachings are daily repeated in the Press. Whole columns are filled up with minutest records of parliamentary debates, of movements of political persons; and, while reading these columns, we too often forget that there is an immense body of men—mankind, in fact—growing and dying, living in happiness or sorrow, labouring and consuming, thinking and creating, besides those few men whose importance has been so swollen up as to overshadow humanity.

And yet, if we revert from the printed matter to our real life and cast a broad glance on society as it is, we are struck with the infinitesimal part played by government in our life. Millions of human beings live and die without having had anything to do with government. Every day millions of transactions are made without the slightest interference of government; and those who enter into agreements have not the slightest intention of breaking bargains. Nay, those agreements which are not protected by government (those of the Exchange or card debts)[24] are perhaps better kept than any others. The simple habit of keeping one's word, the desire of not losing confidence, are quite sufficient in an overwhelming majority of cases to enforce the keeping of agreements. Of course, it may be said that there is still the government which might enforce them if necessary. But not to speak of the numberless cases which could not even be brought before a court, everybody who has the slightest acquaintance with trade will undoubtedly confirm the assertion that, if there were not so strong a feeling of honour in keeping agreements, trade itself would become utterly impossible. Even those merchants and manufacturers who feel not the slightest remorse when poisoning their customers with all kinds of abominable drugs, duly labelled, even they also keep their commercial agreements. But, if such a relative morality as commercial honesty exists now, under the present conditions, when enrichment is the chief motive, the same feeling will further develop very fast as soon as robbing somebody of the fruits of his labour is no longer the economical basis of our life.

**

Another striking feature of our century tells in favour of the same no-government tendency. It is the steady enlargement of the field covered by private initiative, and the recent growth of large organisations resulting merely and simply from free agreement. The railway net of Europe—a confederation of so

---

24 Contracts made in commercial Exchanges and debts incurred by gambling have generally not been enforceable under English law. (Editor)

many scores of separate societies—and the direct transport of passengers and merchandise over so many lines which were built independently and federated together, without even so much as a Central Board of European Railways, are a most striking instance of what is already done by mere agreement. If fifty years ago somebody had predicted that railways built by so many separate companies finally would constitute so perfect a net as they do today, he surely would have been treated as a fool. It would have been urged that so many companies, prosecuting their own interests, would never agree without an International Board of Railways, supported by an International Convention of the European States and endowed with governmental powers. But no such board was resorted to, and the agreement came nevertheless. The Dutch *Beurden*, or associations of ship and boat owners, extending now their organisations over the rivers of Germany, and even to the shipping trade of the Baltic; the numberless amalgamated manufacturers' associations and the *syndicates* of France are so many instances in point. If it be argued that many of these organisations are organisations for exploitation, that proves nothing, because if men prosecuting their own egotistic, often very narrow, interests can agree together, better inspired men, compelled to be more closely connected with other groups, will necessarily agree still easier and still better.

But there also is no lack of free organisations for nobler pursuits. One of the noblest achievements of our century is undoubtedly the Lifeboat Association. Since its first humble start, which we all remember, it has saved no less than thirty-two thousand human lives. It makes appeal to the noblest instincts of man; its activity is entirely dependent upon devotion to the common cause; while its internal organisation is entirely based upon the independence of the local committees. The Hospitals Association and hundreds of like organisations, operating on a large scale and covering each a wide field, may also be mentioned under this head. But, while we know everything about governments and their deeds, what do we know about the results achieved by free co-operation? Thousands of volumes have been written to record the acts of governments; the most trifling amelioration due to law has been recorded; its good effects have been exaggerated, its bad effects passed by in silence. But where is the book recording what has been achieved by free co-operation of well-inspired men? At the same time, hundreds of societies are constituted every day for the satisfaction of some of the infinitely varied needs of civilised man. We have societies for all possible kinds of studies—some of them embracing the whole field of natural science, others limited to a small special branch; societies for gymnastics, for shorthand-writing, for the study of a separate author, for games and all kinds of sports, for forwarding the science of maintaining life and for favouring the art of destroy-ing it; philosophical and industrial, artistic and anti-artistic; for serious work and for mere amusement—in short, there is not a single direction in which men exercise their facul-ties without combining together for the prosecution of some common aim. Every day new societies are formed, while every year the old ones aggregate together into larger units, federate across the national frontiers and co-operate in some common work.

The most striking feature of these numberless free growths is that they continually encroach on what was formerly the domain of the State or the municipality. A householder in a Swiss village on the banks of Lake Léman[25] belongs now to, at least, a dozen different societies which supply him with what is considered elsewhere as a function of the municipal govern-ment. Free federation of independent communes for temporary or permanent purposes lies at the very bottom of Swiss life, and to these federations many a part of Switzerland is indebted for its roads and fountains, its rich vineyards, well-kept forests

25   Better known as Lake Geneva by English-speaking peoples. (Editor)

and meadows which the foreigner admires. And besides these small societies, substituting themselves for the State within some limited sphere, do we not see other societies doing the same on a much wider scale? Each German *Bürger* is proud of the German army, but few of them know how much of its strength is borrowed from the numberless private societies for military studies, exercises and games; and how few are those who understand that their army would become an incoherent mass of men the day that each soldier was no longer inspired by the feelings which inspire him now? In this country, even the task of defending the territory—that is, the chief, the great function of the State—has been undertaken by an army of Volunteers, and this army surely might stand against any army of slaves obeying a military despot. More than that: a private society for the defence of the coasts of England has been seriously spoken of. Let it only come into life, and surely it will be a more effective weapon for self-defence than the ironclads of the navy. One of the most remarkable societies, however, which has recently arisen is undoubtedly the Red Cross Society. To slaughter men on the battlefields, that remains the duty of the State; but these very States recognise their inability to take care of their own wounded: they abandon the task to a great extent to private initiative. What a deluge of mockeries would not have been cast over the poor 'Utopist' who should have dared to say twenty-five years ago that the care of the wounded might be left to private societies! 'Nobody would go into the dangerous places! Hospitals would gather where there was no need of them! National rivalries would result in the poor soldiers dying without any help and so on'—such would have been the outcry. The war of 1871 has shown how perspicacious those prophets are who never believe in human intelligence, devotion and good sense.

***

These facts—so numerous and so customary that we pass by without even noticing them—are in our opinion one of the most prominent features of the second half of our century. The just-mentioned organisms grew up so naturally; they so rapidly extended and so easily aggregated together; they are such unavoidable outgrowths of the multiplication of needs of the civilised man, and they so well replace State-interference, that we must recognise in them a growing factor of our life. Modern progress is really towards the free aggregation of free individuals so as to supplant government in all those functions which formerly were entrusted to it, and which it mostly performed so badly.

As to parliamentary rule, and representative government altogether, they are rapidly falling into decay. The few philosophers who already have shown their defects have only timidly summed up the growing public discontent. It is becoming evident that it is merely stupid to elect a few men and to entrust them with the task of making laws on all possible subjects, of which subjects most of them are utterly ignorant. It is becoming understood that Majority rule is as defective as any other kind of rule; and humanity searches and finds new channels for resolving the pending questions. The Postal Union did not elect an international postal parliament in order to make laws for all postal organisations adherent to the Union. The railways of Europe did not elect an international railway parliament in order to regulate the running of the trains and the repartition of the income of international traffic; and the meteorological and geological societies of Europe did not elect either meteorological or geological parliaments to plan polar stations or to establish a uniform subdivision of geological formations and a uniform colouration of geological maps. They proceeded by means of agreements. To agree together they resorted to congresses; but while sending delegates to their congresses, they did not elect MPs *bons à tout faire*; they did not say to them, 'Vote about everything you like—we shall obey'.

They put questions and discussed them first themselves; then they sent delegates acquainted with the special question to be discussed at the congress, and they sent *delegates*—not rulers. Their delegates returned from the congress with no *laws* in their pockets but with *proposals of agreements*. Such is the way assumed now (the very old way, too) for dealing with questions of public interest—not the way of law making by means of a representative government. Representative government has accomplished its historical mission; it has given a mortal blow to Court rule; and by its debate it has awakened public interest in public questions. But to see in it the government of the future Socialist society is to commit a gross error. Each economical phase of life implies its own political phase; and it is impossible to touch the very basis of the present economical life—private property—without a corresponding change in the very basis of the political organisation. Life already shows in which direction the change will be made. Not in increasing the powers of the State but in restoring to free organisation and free federation in all those branches which are now considered as attributes of the State.

***

The objections to the above may be easily foreseen. It will be said, of course: 'But what is to be done with those who do not keep their agreements? What with those who are not inclined to work? What with those who would prefer breaking the written laws of society, or—in the Anarchist hypothesis—its unwritten customs? Anarchy may be good for a higher humanity—not for the men of our own times'.

First of all, there are two kinds of agreements: there is the free one which is entered upon by free consent, as a free choice between different courses equally open before each of the agreeing parties; and there is the enforced agreement, imposed by one party upon the other and accepted by the latter from sheer necessity; in fact, it is no agreement at all; it is a mere submission to necessity. Unhappily, the great bulk of what are now described as agreements belong to the latter category. When a workman sells his labour to an employer and knows perfectly well that some part of the value of his produce will be unjustly taken by the employer; when he sells it without even the slightest guarantee of being employed so much as six consecutive months—and he is compelled to do so, because he and his family would otherwise starve next week—it is a sad mockery to call that a free contract. Modern economists may call it free, but the father of political economy—Adam Smith—was never guilty of such a misrepresentation. As long as three-quarters of humanity are compelled to enter into agreements of that description, force is, of course, necessary, both to enforce the supposed agreements and to maintain such a state of things. Force—and a good deal of force—is necessary for preventing the labourers from taking possession of what they consider unjustly appropriated by the few; and force is necessary to continually bring new 'uncivilised nations' under the same conditions. The Spencerian no-force party perfectly well understand that; and while they advocate no force for changing the existing conditions, they advocate still more force than is now used for maintaining them. As to Anarchy, it is obviously as incompatible with plutocracy as with any other kind of *cracy*.

But we do not see the necessity of force for enforcing agreements freely entered upon. We never heard of a penalty imposed on a man who belonged to the crew of a lifeboat and at a given moment preferred to abandon the association. All that his comrades would do with him, if he were guilty of a gross neglect, would be probably to refuse to do anything further with him. Nor did we hear of fines imposed on a contributor of Mr. Murray's Dictionary[26] for a delay in his work or of *gen-*

---

26   Sir James Augustus Henry Murray (1837–1915) was a Scottish lexicog-
     rapher and the primary editor of the *Oxford English Dictionary* from 1879

darmes driving the volunteers of Garibaldi to the battlefield. Free agreements need not be enforced.

As to the so-often repeated objection that nobody would labour if he were not compelled to do so by sheer necessity, we heard enough of it before the emancipation of slaves in America, as well as before the emancipation of the serfs in Russia; and we have had the opportunity of appreciating it at its just value. So we shall not try to convince those who can be convinced only by accomplished facts. As to those who reason, they ought to know that if it really was so with some parts of humanity at its lowest stage—and yet, what do we know about it?—or if it is so with some small communities or separate individuals brought to sheer despair by ill-success in their struggle against unfavourable conditions, it is not so with the bulk of the civilised nations. With us, work is a habit and idleness an artificial growth. Of course, when to be a manual worker means to be compelled to work all one's lifelong for ten hours a day, and often more, at producing some part of something—a pin's head, for instance;[27] when it means to be paid wages on which a family can live only on the condition of the strictest limitation of all its needs; when it means to be always under the menace of being thrown tomorrow out of employment—and we know how frequent are the industrial crises and what misery they imply; when it means, in a very great number of cases, premature death in a paupers' hospital,

---

until his death. (Editor)

27 A reference to the opening chapter of Adam Smith's *The Wealth of Nations*, which celebrates the productive power of the division of labour. In a later chapter, Smith recognises the harmful effect of such division on those subject to it and urges public education to help remedy the matter. Kropotkin is reflecting similar comments made by Proudhon in Chapter III of *System of Economic Contradictions* and both recognised the need for workers to control their own workplaces in order to overcome and mitigate the problems associated with the division of labour, problems undoubtedly made worse by capitalist hierarchical relations of production. (Editor)

if not in the workhouse; when to be a manual worker signifies to wear a lifelong stamp of inferiority in the eyes of those very people who live on the work of their 'hands'; when it always means the renouncement of all those higher enjoyments that science and art give to man—oh, then there is no wonder that everybody—the manual worker as well—has but one dream: that of rising to a condition where others would work for him. When I see writers who boast that they are the workers and write that the manual workers are an inferior race of lazy and improvident fellows, I must ask them: Who, then, has made all you see round about you: the houses you live in, the chairs, the carpets, the streets you enjoy, the clothes you wear? Who built the universities where you were taught, and who provided you with food during your school years? And what would become of your readiness to 'work', if you were compelled to work in the above conditions all your life at a pin's head? No doubt, anyhow, *you* would be reported as a lazy fellow! And I affirm that no intelligent man can be closely acquainted with the life of the European working classes without wondering, on the contrary, at their readiness to work, even under such abominable conditions.

Overwork is repulsive to human nature—not work. Overwork for supplying the few with luxury—not work for the well-being of all. Work, labour, is a physiological necessity, a necessity of spending accumulated bodily energy, a necessity which is health and life itself. If so many branches of useful work are so reluctantly done now, it is merely because they mean overwork, or they are improperly organised. But we know—old Franklin knew it[28]—that four hours of useful

---

28 Benjamin Franklin (1706–1790) was one of the Founding Fathers of the United States. A noted polymath, he was a leading author, political theorist, politician and, as a scientist, a major figure in the American Enlightenment. In a letter to Benjamin Vaughn, dated July 1784, he argued that it had 'been computed by some political arithmetician that if every man and woman would work for four hours each day on something useful, that labour would produce sufficient to procure all

work every day would be more than sufficient for supplying everybody with comfort of a moderately well-to-do middle-class house, if we all gave ourselves to productive work, and if we did not waste our productive powers as we do waste them now. As to the childish question, repeated for fifty years: 'Who would do disagreeable work?' Frankly I regret that none of our *savants* has ever been brought to do it, be it for only one day in his life. If there is still work which is really disagreeable in itself, it is only because our scientific men have never cared to consider the means of rendering it less so: they have always known that there were plenty of starving men who would do it for a few pence a day.

***

As to the third—the chief—objection, which maintains the necessity of a government for punishing those who break the law of society, there is so much to say about it that it hardly can be touched incidentally.[29] The more we study the question, the more we are brought to the conclusion that society itself is responsible for the anti-social deeds perpetrated in its midst; and that no punishments, no prisons and no hangmen can diminish the numbers of such deeds; nothing short of a re-organisation of society itself. Three-quarters of all the acts which are brought every year before our courts have their origin, either directly or indirectly, in the present disorganised state of society with regard to the production and distribution of wealth—not in the perversity of human nature. As to the relatively few anti-social deeds which result from anti-social

---

the necessaries and comforts of life, Want and Misery would be banished out of the World, and the rest of the 24 hours might be leisure and happiness'; 'On Luxury, Idleness, and Industry', in *The Works of Dr. Benjamin Franklin* (Boston: T. Bedlington, 1825), 213. (Editor)

29 Some more upon this subject is said in the last two chapters of *In Russian and French Prisons*.

inclinations of separate individuals, it is not by prisons, nor even by resorting to the hangman, that we can diminish their numbers. By our prisons, we merely multiply them and render them worse. By our detectives, our 'price of blood', our executions and our jails, we spread in society such a terrible flow of basest passions and habits, that he who would realise the effects of these institutions to their full extent would be frightened by what society is doing under the pretext of maintaining morality. We *must* search for other remedies, and the remedies have been indicated long since.

Of course, now, when a mother in search of food and shelter for her children must pass by shops filled up with the most refined delicacies of refined gluttony; when gorgeous and insolent luxury is displayed side by side with the most execrable misery; when the dog and the horse of a rich man are far better cared for than millions of children whose mothers earn a pitiful salary in the pit or the manufactory; when each 'modest' evening dress of a lady represents eight months or one year of human labour; when enrichment at somebody else's expense is the avowed aim of the 'upper classes', and no distinct boundary can be traced between honest and dishonest means of making money—then force is the only means for maintaining such a state of things; then an army of policemen, judges and hangmen becomes a necessary institution.

But if all our children—all children are *our* children— received a sound instruction and education—and we have the means of giving it; if every family lived in a decent home—and they *could* at the present high pitch of our production; if every boy and girl were taught a handicraft at the same time as he or she receives scientific instruction, and *not* to be a manual producer of wealth were considered a token of inferiority; if men lived in closer contact with one another and had continually to come into contact on those public affairs which now are invested in the few; and if, in consequence of a closer contact, we were brought to take as lively an interest in our neighbours'

difficulties and pains as we formerly took in those of our kins-
folk—then we should not resort to policemen and judges, to
prisons and executions. Anti-social deeds would be nipped
in the bud, not punished; the few contests which would arise
would be easily settled by arbitrators; and no more force would
be necessary to impose their decisions than is required now for
enforcing the decisions of the family tribunals of China or of
the Valencia water-courts.

***

And here we are brought to consider a great question: What
would become of morality in a society which recognised no
laws and proclaimed the full freedom of the individual? Our
answer is plain. Public morality is independent from and anterior to law and religion. Until now, the teachings of morality
have been associated with religious teachings. But the influence which religious teachings formerly exercised on the mind
has faded of late, and the sanction which morality derived from
religion has no longer the power it formerly had. Millions and
millions grow in our cities who have lost the old faith. Is it a
reason for throwing morality overboard and for treating it with
the same sarcasm as primitive cosmogony?

Obviously not. No society is possible without certain
principles of morality generally recognised. If everybody grew
accustomed to deceive his fellow-man; if we never could rely
on each other's promise and words; if everybody treated his
fellow as an enemy, against whom every means of warfare is
justifiable—no society could exist. And we see, in fact, that
notwithstanding the decay of religious beliefs, the principles
of morality remain unshaken. We even see irreligious people
trying to raise the current standard of morality. The fact is
that moral principles are independent of religious beliefs:
they are anterior to them. The primitive Chuckchis have no
religion: they have only superstitions and fear of the hostile

forces of nature;[30] and nevertheless we find with them the very same principles of morality which are taught by Christians and Buddhists, Mussulmans[31] and Hebrews. Nay, some of their practices imply a much higher standard of tribal morality than that which appears in our civilised society. In fact, each new religion takes its moral principles from the only real stock of morality—the moral habits which grow with men as soon as they unite to live together in tribes, cities or nations. No animal society is possible without resulting in a growth of certain moral habits of mutual support, and even self-sacrifice, for the common well-being. These habits are a necessary condition for the welfare of the species in its struggle for life—co-operation of individuals being a much more important factor in the struggle for the preservation of the species than the so-much-spoken-of physical struggle between individuals for the means of existence. The 'fittest' in the organic world are those who grow accustomed to life in society; and life in society necessarily implies moral habits. As to mankind, it has, during its long existence, developed in its midst a nucleus of social habits, of moral habits, which cannot disappear as long as human societies exist. And therefore, notwithstanding the influence to the contrary which are now at work in consequence of our present economical relations, the nucleus of our moral habits continues to exist. Law and religion only formulate them and endeavour to enforce them by their sanction.

Whatever the variety of theories of morality, all can be brought under three chief categories: the morality of religion; the utilitarian morality; and the theory of moral habits resulting from the very needs of life in society. Each religious morality

---

30 The Chukchi are an indigenous people inhabiting the Chukchi Peninsula, the eastern-most peninsula of Asia. Part of the Russian Empire when Kropotkin was writing, they are now part of the Russian Federation. Kropotkin also mentions them in his 1889 pamphlet *Anarchist Morality*. (Editor)

31 A dated term for Muslims. (Editor)

sanctifies its prescriptions by making them originate from revelation; and it tries to impress its teachings on the mind by a promise of reward or punishment, either in this or in a future life. The utilitarian morality maintains the idea of reward, but it finds it in man himself. It invites men to analyse their pleasures, to clarify them and to give preference to those which are most intense and most durable. We must recognise, however, that, although it has exercised some influence, this system has been judged too artificial by the great mass of human beings. And finally—whatever its varieties—there is the third system of morality which sees in moral actions—in those actions which are most powerful in rendering men best fitted to life in society—a mere necessity of the individual to enjoy the joys of his brethren, to suffer when some of his brethren are suffering; a habit and a second nature, slowly elaborated and perfected by life in society. That is the morality of mankind; and that is also the morality of Anarchy.

I could not better illustrate the difference between the three systems of morality than by repeating the following example. Suppose a child is drowning in a river, and three men stand on the bank of the river: the religious moralist, the utilitarian, and the plain man of the people. The religious man is supposed, first, to say to himself that to save the child would bring him happiness in this or another life, and then save the child; but if he does so, he is merely a good reckoner, no more. Then comes the utilitarian, who is supposed to reason thus: 'The enjoyment of life may be of the higher and of the lower description. To save the child would assure me the higher enjoyment. Therefore, let me jump in the river'. But, admitting that there ever was a man who reasoned in this way, again, he would be a mere reckoner, and society would do better not to rely very much upon him: who knows what sophism might pass one day through his head! And here is the third man. He does not calculate much. But he has grown in the habit of always feeling the joys of those who surround him and to feel happy when others are happy; of suffering, deeply suffering when others suffer. To act accordingly is his second nature. He hears the cry of the mother, he sees the child struggling for life and he jumps into the river like a good dog and saves the child, thanks to the energy of his feelings. And when the mother thanks him, he answers: 'Why! I could not do otherwise than I did'. That is the real morality. That is the morality of the masses of the people; the morality grown to a habit, which will exist, whatever the ethical theories made by philosophers, and will steadily improve in proportion as the conditions of our social life are improved. Such a morality needs no laws for its maintenance. It is a natural growth favoured by the general sympathy which every advance towards a wider and higher morality finds in all fellow men.[32]

Such are, in a very brief summary, the leading principles of Anarchy. Each of them hurts many a prejudice, and yet each of them results from an analysis of the very tendencies displayed by human society. Each of them is rich in consequences and implies a thorough revision of many a current opinion. And Anarchy is not a mere insight into a remote future. Already now, whatever the sphere of action of the individual, he can act either in accordance with Anarchist principles or on an opposite line. And all that may be done in that direction will be done in the direction whereto further development goes. All that may be done in the opposite way will be an attempt to force humanity to go where it will *not* go.

---

32 Kropotkin returned to the subject of ethics soon after this essay, writing a series of article on the subject for *Le Révolté* which were later turned into a pamphlet. These were translated as 'Anarchist Morality' in *Freedom* between October 1891 and July 1892, before being issued as a pamphlet of the same name in 1892. It is included in an edited form in both *Anarchism: A Collection of Revolutionary Writings* (Mineola, NY: Dover Books, 2003) and *Fugitive Writings* (Montréal: Black Rose, 1993). His final years were spent on this, as can be seen by the posthumously published *Ethics: Origin and Development*. (Editor)

■ IAIN MCKAY'S BIBLIOGRAPHICAL NOTES TO 'ANARCHIST COMMUNISM: ITS BASIS AND PRINCIPLES'

Most of Kropotkin's pamphlets were either chapters from his anarchist books or were articles in anarchist newspapers that later became chapters of his books. 'Anarchist Communism: Its Basis and Principles' was one of the few exceptions. It first appeared as two articles written for a leading British journal of liberal thought, *The Nineteenth Century*, in 1887. The first, entitled 'The Scientific Basis of Anarchy', appeared in February and the second, 'The Coming Anarchy', in August, with a note explaining that it had 'been delayed in consequence of the illness of the author'.

These were included (without footnotes) by Albert Parsons (1848–1887) in his 1887 collection *Anarchism: Its Philosophy and Scientific Basis as Defined by Some of Its Apostles*, along with contributions from his fellow Haymarket martyrs and other anarchists, including 'An Anarchist on Anarchy' by Élisée Reclus (1830–1905). Both parts were finally united and revised in 1891 by Kropotkin in a pamphlet entitled *Anarchist Communism: Its Basis and Principles* (Freedom Pamphlet no. 4), which has been reprinted many times, most recently in 1987.[1] It has also appeared in many languages—into French for the journal *La*

---

1   The 1987 edition was published by Freedom Press and edited by Nicholas Walter. This edition has utiltised some of his end notes.

Société nouvelle: Revue Internationale as 'Les Bases scientifiques de l'anarchie', in 1888, and 'L'Inévitable Anarchie', in 1895—and in many anthologies. Sadly, the most easily accessible version of this text—included in *Anarchism: A Collection of Revolutionary Writings* (Mineola, NY: Dover Books, 2003) and *Fugitive Writings* (Montréal: Black Rose, 1993)—is substantially edited (without indicating so), with more than a quarter of the original removed. It is reprinted in full here.

This is the fate of the pamphlet, but what of its origins? Why did a leading anarchist revolutionary find the opportunity to expound his ideas to a predominantly middle-class British audience?

Kropotkin was friends with the editor of *The Nineteenth Century*, James Knowles (1831–1908), whom he first met during a year-long stay in Britain, after being expelled from Switzerland in 1881. By this time, Kropotkin had achieved some international fame for rejecting his title and position, his arrest for radical agitation in 1874, followed by imprisonment in the infamous Peter and Paul Fortress and a daring escape from its hospital in 1876. As a result, Knowles asked Kropotkin for articles on the Russian penal system. However, these appeared after Kropotkin was arrested in France in December 1882 as part of a wave of repression against anarchists in the Lyons area.[2]

After a trial in 1883, which the accused anarchists used to propagate their ideas, Kropotkin was sentenced to five years in prison. As the result of an international campaign for amnesty for him and his comrades, which drew support from many influential and famous people across the globe, he was released in 1886 and left France for Britain, where he remained in exile until he returned to Russia after the February Revolution of 1917.

---

2   Kropotkin's book *In Russian and French Prisons* (1887) included these articles as well as others published in *The Nineteenth Century* on his experience of imprisonment in France, along with his discussion of the counter-productive role of prisons and what should replace them for dealing with the anti-social actions of the few.

As well as helping to found the anarchist newspaper *Freedom* in 1886 and contributing many articles to it (see *Act for Yourselves* [London: Freedom Press, 1987] for a collection of these texts), he also sought an income ('A socialist must always rely upon his own work for his living', as he put it in his *Memoirs*). Among other things, this led him to re-establish his relationship with Knowles, writing 'In French Prisons' for *The Nineteenth Century* (March 1886)—these and his earlier writings on the Russian penal system were incorporated into the book *In Russian and French Prisons* (1887). Kropotkin then contributed articles on various subjects (mostly science-related but sometimes political) until 1919. *Mutual Aid* (1902) and *Fields, Factories and Workshops* (1898, 1912) first appeared as articles in *The Nineteenth Century*, before being revised and collected as books.

With the Lyons trial and his well-reported part in the defence, Kropotkin's exile in Britain was an obvious opportunity for Knowles to get an account of communist anarchist ideas for his readership. Kropotkin happily obliged, tailoring his articles to an audience unfamiliar with anarchist ideas by relating them to those that his readers *were* familiar with: British liberalism and State Socialism. In other words, rearticulating libertarian politics in the language of British radicalism.

He did so by comparing anarchist ideas with the arguments of those most associated with opposing State interference, at least in rhetoric. This was classical liberalism, in the shape of Herbert Spencer (1820–1903). Spencer is now a mostly forgotten figure, remembered best if at all—outside the so-called right-wing 'libertarians' (better termed propertarians),[3] who claim him as one of their precursors—for coining the phrase 'survival of the fittest', but when Kropotkin was writing he was

---

3 For a discussion of the socialist history of 'libertarian' and its attempted appropriation by the American far right, see my '160 Years of Libertarian', *Anarcho-Syndicalist Review* no. 71–72 (Fall 2017).

a well-known intellectual.[4] A strict classical liberal, he opposed all forms of State intervention beyond the defence of property and justified his ideas with reference to evolutionary theory: a social Darwinist, in short. Likewise, Kropotkin referred to the ideas of State Socialism in the shape of social democracy, then on the rise in Germany. He also critiqued the commonplace platitude within polite middle-class circles, derived from the work of Thomas Robert Malthus (1766–1834), that the misery of the working class was due purely to the population growing faster than the means of subsistence.[5]

In this way, Kropotkin tailored his article to his audience, contrasting anarchism to the two sets of ideas he knew they were aware of and indicating what anarchism shared with them. This could give the impression that anarchism was somehow a mishmash of these two ideologies. That is not the case, as can be seen from Kropotkin not using such terminology elsewhere. Indeed, a close reading of 'Anarchist Communism' shows that his argument is that classical liberalism *cannot* reach its goal of minimising the State because of its support for private property: the inequalities in wealth and power this produced needed the few to be protected against the many, necessitating a State. More, a society marked by hierarchy—relations of master-servant—within production, as capitalism is, cannot be a free one, and replacing the boss with the bureaucrat changes little. Hence the need for economic *and*

---

4   Given this, unsurprisingly Kropotkin returned to Spencer's ideas again: 'Co-operation: A Reply to Herbert Spencer', *Freedom*, December 1896 and January 1897; a sympathetic obituary in Les *Temps Nouveaux* and *Freedom* (1904) later included as an appendix of *La science moderne et l'anarchie* (1913), chapter VI of *Modern Science and Anarchism* (1912) and chapter XII of the posthumous *Ethics: Origin and Development* (1924). All bar the last are included in the *Modern Science and Anarchy* (Edinburgh: AK Press, 2018), while Kropotkin's critique of his ideas is discussed in its introduction.

5   Kropotkin returned to Malthus during his discussion of the 'Possibilities of Agriculture' in Chapter IV of *Fields, Factories and Workshops*.

political freedom—rooted in an egalitarian (socialist) critique of both State and capital.

The rise of neo-liberalism shows the accuracy of Kropotkin's critique, with the era which commenced under Thatcher and Reagan being marked by freer markets but stronger States. Similarly, the failure of State Socialism also confirmed Kropotkin's predictions that it would be little more than State capitalism. Finally, his short but devastating critique of Malthus and his 'law of population'—building on Proudhon's critique in the sadly still untranslated second volume of *System of Economic Contradictions* (1846)—has been confirmed time and time again.

As well as this, it provides an excellent summary of anar-chist communism and addresses the most common objections to this viable and attractive alternative to capitalism. Little wonder it became a classic of libertarian thought.

■ THE STATE: ITS HISTORIC ROLE

I

By taking the *State and its historic role* as the subject for this study, I believe I am responding to a deeply felt need at the present time: that of exploring the very concept of the State, of studying its essence, its past role and the part it may be called upon to play in the future.

It is above all on the question of the State that Socialists are divided. Two main currents emerge in the all of the factions that exist amongst us which correspond to different temperaments, different ways of thinking and above all in the degree of confidence in the forthcoming revolution.

There are those, on the one hand, who hope to accomplish the social revolution through the State: to preserve most of its powers, to even extend them, to use them for the revolution. And there are those who, like us, see in the State, not only in its present form but in its very essence and in all the forms that it may take, an obstacle to the social revolution: the greatest hindrance to the birth of a society based on equality and freedom, the historic form developed to prevent this blossoming. They work to abolish the State, not to reform it.

The division, as we see, is deep. It corresponds with two divergent currents which are encountered in all the philosophy, literature and action of our time. And if the prevailing notions on the State remain as obscure as they are today, it will be, without a doubt, upon this question that the most obstinate struggles will be waged when—soon, hopefully—Communist ideas seek their practical realisation in the life of societies.

It is therefore important, after having so often criticised the current State, to seek the reason for its emergence, to go deeper into the role it has played in the past, to compare it with the institutions that it has replaced.

Let us first agree on what we want we mean by the term State.

There is, as is well-known, the German school which likes to confuse *the State* with *Society*. This confusion is to be found amongst the best German thinkers and many of the French who cannot conceive of society without statist concentration: and this is why Anarchists are usually reproached for wanting to 'destroy society', of preaching the return to 'the permanent war of each against all'.

However, to think that way is to completely ignore the advances made in the domain of history during the past thirty years; it is to ignore [the fact] that man lived in societies for thousands of years before he knew of the State; it is to forget that for the European nations the State is of recent origin—that it barely dates from the sixteenth century; it is, finally, to disregard that the most glorious periods of humanity were those in which liberties and local life were not yet destroyed by the State, and in which large numbers of men lived in communes and free federations.

The State is only one of the forms taken by society during the course of history. How can we confuse the permanent and the accidental?

In addition, some have also confused *State* with *Government*. Since there can be no State without government, it has sometimes been said that it is the absence of government, not the abolition of the State, that must be aimed for.

However, it seems to me that in the State and government we have two concepts of a different order. The idea of the

State implies something quite different from the idea of government. It not only includes the existence of a power placed above society, but also of a *territorial concentration* and a *concentration of many functions in the life of societies in the hands of a few*. It implies some new relationships between members of society which did not exist before the formation of the State. A whole mechanism of legislation and of policing is developed to subject some classes to the domination of other classes.

This distinction, which at first sight might not be obvious, emerges especially when we study the origins of the State.

Moreover, there is only one way of really understanding the State: it is to study its historic development, and this is what we shall try to do.

The Roman Empire was a State in the real sense of the word. To this day it remains the ideal of the jurist.

Its organs covered a vast domain with a tight network. Everything flowed towards Rome: economic life, military life, judicial reports, wealth, education and even religion. From Rome came the laws, the magistrates, the legions to defend the territory, the prefects,[1] the gods. The whole life of the Empire went back to the Senate—later to Caesar, the omnipotent, omniscient, god of the Empire. Every province, every district had its Capitol in miniature, its small portion of Roman sovereignty to direct every aspect of its life. A single law, the law imposed by Rome, prevailed in the Empire; and this empire did not represent a confederation of fellow citizens: it was simply a herd of *subjects*.

Even now, the jurist and the authoritarian still admire the unity of that Empire, the unitarian spirit of its laws, the beauty—they say—[and] the harmony of that organisation.[2]

---

1   Prefects (Latin: *Praefectus*) were military or civil officials in the Roman Empire whose authority was conferred by a higher authority. (Editor)

2   The term *unitarian* refers to a regime that was centralised, indivisible and constituted into a homogeneous single unit (*unitaire*). Proudhon popularised opposition to this system in such works as *The Federative Principle* (1863). (Editor)

But the disintegration from within, hastened by the barbarian invasion; the extinction of local life, which could no longer resist the attacks from outside nor the gangrene spreading from the centre, the domination by the rich who had appropriated the land [for themselves] and the misery of those who cultivated it—all these causes tore the Empire apart, and on its ruins a new civilisation developed which is ours today.

And if, leaving aside the civilisation of antiquity, we study the origins and developments of this young barbarian civilisation until the times when, in its turn, it gave birth to our modern States, we will be able to grasp the essence of the State. We shall grasp it better than had we embarked on the study of the Roman Empire, or that of Alexander of Macedonia, or even the despotic monarchies of the East.

By taking these powerful barbarian demolishers of the Roman Empire as our point of departure, we can trace the evolution of our entire civilisation from its beginnings to the State phase.

II

Most philosophers of the eighteenth century had a very elementary idea of the origin of societies.

At first, they said, men lived in small, isolated families and perpetual war between these families characterised the normal situation. But one fine day, realising at last the inconveniences of their endless struggles, men decided to put themselves into society. A social contract was concluded between the scattered families who willingly submitted themselves to an authority which—need I say?—became the starting point and the initiator of all progress. Is it necessary to add, since we have already been told at school, that our present governments have so far maintained their noble role as the salt of the earth, the peacemakers and civilisers of the human race?

Conceived at the time when we knew little about the origins of man, this idea dominated the eighteenth century; and it must be said that in the hands of the Encyclopaedists and of Rousseau the idea of the 'social contract' became a weapon against the divine rights of royalty. Nevertheless, despite the services it rendered in the past, this theory must be acknowledged as false.

The fact is that all animals, except some carnivores and birds of prey, and some species that are disappearing, live in societies. In the struggle for life, it is the sociable species which prevail over those that are not. In each category of animals, they are at the top of the ladder, and there can be no doubt that the first human-like beings were already living in societies.

Man did not create society; society existed before man.

We now also know—anthropology has convincingly demonstrated it—that the point of departure for humanity was not the family but the clan, the tribe. The patriarchal family as we know it, or as it is depicted in Hebrew traditions, only appeared much later. Man spent tens of thousands of years in the clan or tribal phase—let us call it the primitive or, if you wish, the savage tribe—and man had already developed a whole series of institutions, habits and customs many of which preceded the institutions of the patriarchal family.

In these tribes the separate family no more existed than it exists amongst so many other sociable mammals. Division within the tribe was rather by generations; and from a far distant age, going right back to the dawn of the human race, limitations had been established to prevent sexual relations between different generations, which were allowed [between those] in the same generation. We can still find traces of that period in some contemporary tribes and in the language, customs and superstitions of peoples much more advanced in civilisation.

The whole tribe hunted or gathered in common and, their hunger satisfied, they devoted themselves passionately to their dramatised dances. To this day we still find tribes that are very close to this primitive phase pushed to the peripheries of the large continents or to mountainous regions, the least accessible [parts] of our globe.

The accumulation of private property could not take place there, since anything that had belonged to a particular member of the tribe was destroyed or burned where his body was buried. This is still done, even in England, by the Gypsies, and funeral rites of the 'civilised' still bear the imprint [of this custom]: the Chinese burn paper models of the dead person's possessions, and at the military leader's funeral his horse, his sword, and his decorations accompany him to his grave. The meaning of the institution is lost: but the form has survived.

Far from expressing contempt for human life, these primitive people hated murder and blood. To spill blood was considered so serious that every drop spilled—not only human blood but also that of certain animals—required that the aggressor should lose an equal amount of his own blood.

Furthermore, a murder within the tribe is something *quite unknown*; for example, among the Inuit, or Eskimos—those survivors of the Stone Age who inhabit the Arctic regions— among the Aleutians, etc., we definitely know that there has not been a single murder *within the tribe* for fifty, sixty or more years.

But when tribes of different origin, colour and language met in their migrations, it often ended in war. It is true that even then men sought to pacify these encounters. As Maine, Post and E. Nys have so well demonstrated, tradition was already developing the seeds of what later became international law. For instance, a village could not be attacked without warning the inhabitants. Never would anyone dare to kill on the path used by women to reach the spring. And to make peace it was often necessary to balance the numbers of men killed on both sides.

However, all these precautions and many others besides were not enough: solidarity did not extend beyond the clan or tribe; quarrels arose between people of different clans and tribes, and these quarrels would end in violence and even murder.

Accordingly, a general law began to be developed between the clans and tribes. 'Your members have wounded or killed one of ours; we have a right therefore to kill one of you or to inflict an identical wound on one of you'—it did not matter who, since the tribe was always responsible for the acts of its members. The well-known verses of the Bible: 'Blood for blood, an eye for an eye, a tooth for a tooth, a wound for a wound, a life for a life'—but no more!—as Koenigswarter noted so well, derive their origin from this. It was their concept of justice . . . and we have no reason to feel superior since the principle of 'a life for a life' which prevails in our [legal] codes is only one of many survivals [from the past].

As you can see, a whole series of institutions, and many others I shall not mention, a complete code of tribal morality was already developed during this primitive phase. And to keep this nucleus of sociable customs alive, habit, custom and tradition were enough. There was no authority to impose it.

Primitive people had, without doubt, temporary leaders. The sorcerer, the rainmaker—the scholars of the time—sought to benefit from what they knew or believed they knew about nature to dominate their fellow men. Similarly, he who could more easily memorise the proverbs and songs in which tradition was embodied gained influence. At popular festivals he would recite these proverbs and songs in which were passed on the decisions taken on such-and-such an occasion by the people's assembly in such-and-such a controversy. In many tribes this is still done. And from that age onwards, these 'educated' [people] sought to ensure domination by passing on their knowledge only to the chosen few, the initiated. All religions, and even the arts and crafts, began with 'mysteries'; and modern research shows us the important role secret societies of the initiates play to maintain certain traditional practices in primitive clans. Already the seeds of authority are present there.

It goes without saying that the brave, the audacious and, above all, the wise also became temporary leaders in the conflicts with other tribes or during migrations. But the alliance between the bearer of the 'law' (those who knew by heart tradition and past decisions), the military chief and the sorcerer did not exist; the *State* was no more part of these tribes than it is in a society of bees or ants or amongst our contemporaries the Patagonians and Eskimos.

This phase nevertheless lasted for thousands and thousands of years, and the barbarians who overran the Roman Empire had also gone through it. They had barely emerged from it.

In the early centuries of our era there were widespread migrations of the tribes and confederations of tribes that inhabited Central and Northern Asia. Influxes of tribes, driven by more or less civilised peoples, came down from the high plateaux of Asia—probably driven by the rapid desiccation of these plateaux[3]—spread all over Europe, each driving the other and mixing together in their rush towards the West.

During these migrations, when so many tribes of different origins were mixed, the primitive tribe which still existed amongst most of the savage inhabitants of Europe was bound to disintegrate. The tribe was based on a common origin and the worship of common ancestors; but to which common origin could these agglomerations [of people] appeal when they emerged from the confusion of the migrations, the drives, the intertribal wars, during which here and there we can already see the emergence of the patriarchal family—the nucleus

---

3   The reasons which lead me to this hypothesis are put forward in a paper, *Desiccation of Eur-Asia*, written for the Research Department of the Geographical Society of London, and published in the *Geographical Journal* of the society, June 1904 [vol. 23, no. 6, pp. 722–34].

deriving from the monopolisation of some of the women conquered or abducted from other nearby tribes?

The old ties were broken, and to avoid dispersal (which
happened, in fact, to many tribes, now lost to history) new
[social] ties had to emerge. And they arose. They were found in
the communal possession *of the land*—of the territory on which
each agglomeration had finally settled.[4]

The common possession of a certain territory—of this small
valley, of those hills—became the basis for a new understanding. The ancestor gods had lost all meaning; then local gods, of
that valley, river, forest, came to provide religious blessing to
the new agglomerations, replacing the gods of the primitive
tribe. Later Christianity, always ready to accommodate itself to
pagan survivals [from the past], made them local saints.

Henceforth, the village commune consisting entirely or
partly of distinct families—all united, however, by the common
possession of the land—became the essential common bond
for centuries to come.

Over vast areas of Eastern Europe, Asia and Africa it
still exists. The barbarians—Scandinavians, Germans, Slavs,
etc.—who destroyed the Roman Empire lived under this kind
of organisation. And by studying the barbarian codes of that
period, as well as the confederations of village communes that
exist today amongst the Kabyles, Mongols, Hindus, Africans,
etc., it has been possible to reconstruct in its entirety this form
of society, which signifies the starting point of our present
civilisation.

Let us take a look at this institution.

---

4   Readers interested in this subject, as well as in the communal and free
     cities phases, will find further details and the necessary information
     on the literature of the subject in my *Mutual Aid*, Paris (Hachette), 1900.

III

The village commune consisted, as it still does, of distinct families. But the families of the same village owned the land in common. They considered it as their common heritage and apportioned it according to the size of each family—their needs and their strengths. Hundreds of millions of men still live in this way in Eastern Europe, India, Java, etc. It is the same system that has been established in our time freely in Siberia by Russian peasants once the State gave them a chance to occupy the vast Siberian territory in their own way.

Today the cultivation of the land in a village community is carried out by each household independently. Since all the arable land is distributed between the households (and redistributed when necessary) each cultivates its field as best it can. But originally the land was also worked in common and this custom is still carried on in many places—at least on a part of the land. As to the clearing of woodland and the thinning of forests, the construction of bridges, the building of small forts and towers for use as places of refuge in the event of invasion—all that was done in common, just as hundreds of millions of peasants still do where the village commune has resisted the encroachments of the State. But 'consumption', to use a modern expression, was already taking place by families, each of which having its cattle, its vegetable garden and its provisions. The means for [both] hoarding and for passing down by inheritance accumulated goods had already been introduced.

In all its affairs the village commune was sovereign. Local custom was law and the plenary assembly of all the heads of family, men and women, was the judge, the only judge, in civil and criminal matters. When one of the inhabitants had lodged a complaint against another by sticking his knife in the ground at the place where the commune normally gathered, the commune had to 'find the sentence' according to local custom once the *fact* of an offence had been established by the juries of the two parties in dispute.

If I were to recount all the interesting aspects of this phase, I would not have the space in which to do so. I must therefore refer the reader to *Mutual Aid*. Suffice it to mention here that *all* the institutions which States later seized for the benefit of minorities, all the notions of law that exist in our codes (mutilated for the advantage of minorities) and all the forms of judicial procedure, in so far as they offer guarantees to the individual, originated in the village commune. So when we imagine that we have made a great advance by introducing, for example, the jury, we have only returned to the institution of the so-called 'barbarians' after having changed it to the advantage of the ruling classes. Roman law merely superimposed itself onto customary law.

The sense of national unity was developing at the same time through large free federations of village communes.

The village commune, based on the possession and very often on the cultivation of the land in common, sovereign [both] as judge and legislator of customary law, satisfied most of the needs of social existence.

But not for all its needs: there were still others to be satisfied. But the spirit of the time was not to appeal to a government as soon as a new need made itself felt. It was, on the contrary, to take the initiative yourself, to unite, to join forces, to federate; to create an agreement, large or small, numerous or restricted, which fulfilled the new need. And society then was literally covered, like a network, with sworn brotherhoods; of guilds for mutual support, of 'conjurations', within the village and outwith the village, in the federation.

We can observe this phase and spirit at work even today, amongst many barbarian federations which have remained outside the modern States which are modelled on the Roman or rather Byzantine type.

Thus, to take one example amongst many, the Kabyles have maintained their village commune, with the powers I have just mentioned: land in common, communal tribunal, etc. But man feels the need for action beyond the narrow confines of his hamlet. Some rove the world, seeking adventures as merchants. Others devote themselves to some trade—or 'art'. And these merchants, these artisans, unite into 'brotherhoods', even though they belong to different villages, tribes or confederations. It is necessary to unite for mutual assistance on distant journeys, it is necessary for the mutual exchange of the mysteries of the trade—and they come together. They swear brotherhood and practice it in a way that strikes the European: real brotherhood, and not just in words.

But then, misfortune can happen to anyone. Who knows whether tomorrow, perhaps in a brawl, a normally gentle and quiet man may exceed the established limits of decorum and sociability? Who knows if he might not resort to blows and inflict wounds? It will then be necessary to pay heavy compensation to the insulted or wounded; it will be necessary for him to defend himself before the village assembly and to reconstruct the facts, on the testimony of six, ten or twelve 'sworn brothers'. All the more reason to enter a brotherhood.

Besides, man feels the need to engage in politics, to intrigue, perhaps, to propagate a particular moral opinion or a particular custom. There is, finally, external peace to be safeguarded; alliances with other tribes to be concluded; federations to be constituted far and wide; ideas on intertribal law to be spread. Well then, to satisfy all these needs of an emotional or intellectual nature the Kabyles, the Mongols, the Malays do not appeal to a government; they do not have one. Men of customary law and individual initiative, they have not been impaired from acting for themselves by the corruption of a government and a church. They unite spontaneously. They form sworn brotherhoods, political and religious societies, associations of crafts—*guilds*, as they were called in the Middle Ages, *çofs* as they are called today by the Kabyles. And these *çofs* extend beyond the boundaries of the hamlet; they radiate far into the desert and into foreign cities; and brotherhood is practised in these associations. To refuse help to a member of his *cof*—even at the risk of losing all his possessions and his life—is to commit an act of treason towards the 'brotherhood'; it is to be treated as the murderer of the 'brother'.

What we find today among the Kabyles, Mongols, Malays, etc., was the very essence of life of the barbarians in Europe from the fifth to the twelfth and even until the fifteenth century. Under the name of *guilds, friendships, brotherhoods, universitas,*[5] etc., associations multiplied: for mutual defence, to avenge affronts suffered by some member of the association and to express solidarity, to replace 'eye for an eye' vengeance by compensation, followed by acceptance of the aggressor into the brotherhood; for the exercise of crafts, for aid in case of illness, for defence of the territory; to prevent encroachments of the emerging authority; for commerce, for the practice of 'good neighbourliness'; for propaganda—in a word, for all that Europeans educated by the Rome of the Caesars and the Popes nowadays demand from the State. It is even very doubtful whether there was a single man in that period, free or serf—except those who had been expelled by their own brotherhoods—who did not belong to a brotherhood or some guild in addition to his commune.

The Scandinavian *Sagas* extol their exploits; the devotion of sworn brothers is the theme of the most beautiful poems. Naturally, the Church and emerging kings, representatives of

---

5   The word *universitas* originally applied to the scholastic guilds, a corporation organised for the purposes of higher learning. The word 'university' is derived from the Latin *universitas magistrorum et scholarium*, which roughly means 'community of teachers and scholars'. These medieval universities were established across Europe between the eleventh and fourteenth centuries. (Editor)

the Byzantine (or Roman) law which [also] reappeared, hurled their denunciations and their decrees against these brotherhoods; but fortunately they remained a dead letter.

The whole history of the period loses its meaning, it becomes absolutely incomprehensible, if we do not take into account those brotherhoods, these unions of brothers and sisters, which sprang up everywhere to meet the many needs of the economic and personal lives of man.

To fully grasp the immense progress achieved by this double institution of village communes and freely sworn brotherhoods—outside any Roman, Christian or Statist influence—take Europe as it was at the time of the barbarian invasion and compare it to what it became in the tenth and eleventh centuries. The wild forest is conquered, colonised; villages cover the country and they are surrounded by fields and hedges, protected by small forts, connected to each other by paths crossing forests and marshes.

In these villages you find the seeds of the industrial arts and you discover a whole network of institutions for maintaining internal and external peace. In the event of murder or injury the villagers no longer seek, as previously in the tribe, to slay or to inflict an equivalent wound on the aggressor or one of his kin or his fellow villagers. Rather is it the brigand-lords who still adhere to that principle (hence their endless wars); whereas between villagers *compensation*, fixed by arbiters, becomes the rule; after which peace is re-established and the aggressor is often, if not always, adopted by the family who was wronged by his aggression.

Arbitration for all disputes becomes a deeply rooted institution, a daily practice—in spite of and against the bishops and the emerging kinglets who would like every difference to be laid before them or their agents, in order to benefit from the *fred*—a fine once levied by the village on the violators of the public peace in every dispute and which the kings and bishops now appropriated.

Finally, hundreds of villages are already united in powerful federations sworn to internal peace, that consider their territory as a common heritage and are united for mutual defence. These were the seeds of European *nations*. And to this day we can still study these federations in action amongst Mongolian, Turko-Finnish[6] and Malayan tribes.

Yet black clouds are gathering on the horizon. Other associations, those of dominant minorities, are also formed, and they seek slowly to transform these free men into serfs, into subjects. Rome is dead; but its tradition is reborn, and the Christian Church, haunted by the visions of Eastern theocracies, gives its powerful support to the new powers that seek to establish themselves.

Far from being the bloodthirsty beast that some wished to make him [in order] to prove the necessity to dominate him, man has always loved quiet, peace. Quarrelsome rather than fierce, he prefers his cattle, his land and his hut to the profession of soldier. This is why, no sooner had the great migrations of barbarians slowed down, no sooner had the hordes and the tribes more or less settled themselves in their respective territories, we see the defence of the territory against new waves of emigrants entrusted to the care of someone who engages a small band of adventurers—hardened warriors or brigands—to follow him while the great mass rears its cattle or works the land. And this defender soon begins to accumulate wealth; he gives horses and iron (then very expensive) to the destitute settler who has neither horse nor plough and enslaves him. He also starts to seize the beginnings of military power.

Moreover, little by little, tradition, which is the law, is forgotten by most. In each village there are hardly any elders who have been able to remember the verses and songs in which are

---

6   A somewhat dated reference to the Khazars, Magyars and other a multi-ethnic conglomerates of semi-nomadic Turkic peoples who lived in an area extending from Eastern Europe to Central Asia. (Editor)

recounted the 'precedents' of which customary law is composed, and who recites them on the days of great festivals before the commune. And, little by little, a few families make it their speciality, transmitted from father to son, to remember these songs and verses, to 'preserve the law' in its purity. Villagers would go to them to adjudicate on complicated disputes, especially when two villages or two confederations could not agree to accept the decisions of the arbiters taken from their midst.

Princely or royal authority is already germinating in these families, and the more I study the institutions of that period the more I see that knowledge of the customary law did much more to establish that authority than the power of the sword. Man let himself be enslaved much more by his desire to 'punish' the aggressor according to 'the law' than by direct military conquest.

And, gradually, the first 'concentration of powers', the first mutual insurance for domination—that of the judge and the military chief—is made against the village community. A single man assumes these two functions. He surrounds himself with armed men to implement judicial decisions; he fortifies himself in his small tower; he accumulates in his family the riches of the time—bread, cattle, iron—and little by little imposes his domination on the peasants in the vicinity.

The scholar of the period, that is to say, the sorcerer or the priest, are not long in lending support to him, to share domination; or, by joining force and knowledge of customary law to his feared wizard power, the priest takes it for himself. Hence, the temporal authority of the bishops in the ninth, tenth and eleventh centuries.

I would need a lecture [in itself] rather than a chapter to thoroughly deal with this subject, so full of new lessons, and to recount how free men gradually became serfs, forced to work for the lord of the manor, secular or clerical; how authority was slowly, hesitantly constituted over villages and boroughs; how the peasants joined together, rebelled, fought to oppose this growing domination; and how they were defeated in those struggles against the stout walls of the castle, against the men clad in iron who defended them.

It is enough for me to say that around the tenth and eleventh centuries Europe seemed to be moving towards the constitution of barbarian kingdoms like those we find today in the heart of Africa or those theocracies we know from Eastern history. This could not happen in a day; but the seeds of those petty royalties and of those petty theocracies were already there; they asserted themselves more and more.

Fortunately, the 'barbarian' spirit—Scandinavian, Saxon, Celt, German, Slav—which had driven men for seven or eight centuries to seek the satisfaction of their needs through individual initiative and the free agreement of brotherhoods and guilds—fortunately this spirit still lived in the villages and boroughs. The barbarians allowed themselves to be enslaved, they laboured for the master, but their spirit of free action and free agreement had not yet been corrupted. Their brotherhoods were more alive than ever, and the crusades had only succeeded in arousing and developing them in the West.

Then the revolution of the urban commune, resulting from the union of the village commune and the sworn brotherhood of the artisan and the merchant—a revolution which had been long prepared by the federal spirit of the time—exploded in the eleventh and twelfth centuries with a striking unity across Europe. It had already begun in the Italian communes during the tenth century.

This revolution, which most university historians prefer to ignore or to underestimate, saved Europe from the disaster which threatened it. It stopped the development of theocratic and despotic kingdoms in which our civilisation would probably have ended up sinking after a few centuries of pompous self-fulfilment, as the civilisations of Mesopotamia, Assyria and Babylon sank. It opened a new phase of life—the phase of free communes.

IV

It is easy to understand why modern historians, trained in the Roman spirit and seeking to trace all institutions back to Rome, have so much difficulty understanding the communalist movement of the eleventh and twelfth centuries. The virile affirmation of the individual which succeeded in constituting society by the free federation of men, villages and cities was the complete negation of the unitarian and centralising Roman spirit by which they seek to explain history in our university education. Nor is it connected to any historical personality or with any central institution.

It is a natural development, belonging, like the tribe and the village commune, to a certain phase in human evolution, and not to any particular nation or region.

This is the reason why university science does not grasp it and why Augustin Thierry and Sismondi, who had understood the spirit of the period, had no continuators in France, where Luchaire is today still the only one to have taken up—more or less—the tradition of the great historian of the Merovingian and communalist periods. This is even why, in England and Germany, the revival of studies into this period and a vague understanding of its spirit are of very recent origin.

The commune of the Middle Ages, the free city, originates, on the one hand, to the village commune and, on the other, to those thousands of brotherhoods and guilds that were formed in that period outwith the territorial union. A federation between these two kinds of unions, it asserted itself under the protection of its fortified enclosing walls and turrets.

In many regions it was a peaceful development. Elsewhere—and this is the rule for Western Europe—it was the result of a revolution. When the inhabitants of a particular borough felt sufficiently protected by their walls, they made a 'conjuration'. They mutually swore an oath to drop all pending matters concerning insults, violence or injuries and swore for the disputes that would arise in the future never to have recourse to any judge other than the syndics which they would nominate themselves. In every good neighbourliness or craft guild, in every sworn brotherhood, it had long been regular practice. In every village community such had been the practice in the past, before the bishop and the kinglet had succeeded in introducing, and later imposing upon it, their judge.

Now, the hamlets and parishes which made up the borough, as well as the guilds and brotherhoods which had developed there, regarded themselves as a single *amitas*, nominated their judges and swore permanent union between all these groups.

A charter was quickly drafted and accepted. If necessary, they sent for a copy of the charter of a neighbouring small commune (today we know of hundreds of these charters) and the commune was formed. The bishop or the prince, who had been up to then the judge in the commune and had often become more or less the master, had thus only to acknowledge the *fait accompli*—or fight the young conjuration with arms. Often the king—that is to say the prince who sought to secure his superiority over the other princes and whose coffers were always empty—'granted' the charter for a fee. He thus renounced his intention of imposing *his* judge on the commune while ensuring his prominence as regards the other feudal lords. But this was by no means the rule: hundreds of communes lived without any ratification other than their goodwill, their ramparts and their spears.

In a hundred years, this movement spread, with a striking unity, throughout Europe—by imitation, note it well, covering Scotland, France, the Netherlands, Scandinavia, Germany, Italy, Poland and Russia. And when we now compare the charters and the internal organisation of the French, English, Scottish, Dutch, Scandinavian, German, Polish, Russian, Swiss, Italian and Spanish communes, we are struck by the close similarity of these charters and the organisation that grew up sheltered by these 'social contracts'. What a striking lesson for the Romanists and the Hegelians who know of no other means than servitude before the law to achieve similarity in institutions!

From the Atlantic to the middle course of the Volga, and from Norway to Sicily, Europe was covered with such communes—some becoming populous cities such as Florence, Venice, Amiens, Nuremberg or Novgorod, others remaining boroughs of a hundred or even twenty families, and yet treated as equals by their more prosperous sisters.

Organisms full of vigour, communes obviously differed in their evolution. The geographical location, the nature of external commerce, the resistance to be overcome from outside, gave each commune its [own] history. But for all the principle is the same. Pskov in Russia and Bruges in Flanders, a Scottish town of three hundred inhabitants and wealthy Venice with its islands, a borough in the north of France or Poland and Florence the Beautiful represent the same *amitas*: the same fellowship of the village communes and guilds, associated within the boundaries of the walls. Their constitution, in its general features, is the same.

Generally, the town whose walls grew longer and thicker with the population and which flanked itself with higher and higher towers, each raised by this neighbourhood or that guild and bearing its individual stamp—generally, I say, the town was divided into four, five or six sections, or districts, which radiated from the citadel or the cathedral towards the walls. By preference these sectors were each inhabited by an 'art' or craft, while the new crafts—the 'young arts'—occupied the suburbs which were soon enclosed by a new fortified wall.

The *street*, or the parish, represented the territorial unit, which corresponded to the earlier village community. Each street, or parish, had its popular assembly, its forum, its popular tribunal, its priest, its militia, its banner and often its seal, symbol of its sovereignty. Federated with other streets it nevertheless retained its independence.

The professional unit, which often merged with the neighbourhood or district, was the guild—the craft association. The latter also had its saints, its assembly, its forum, its judges. It had its funds, its land holdings, its militia and its banner. It also had its seal, emblem of its *sovereignty*. In the event of war, if it judged it appropriate, its militia joined with the other guilds and planted its banner alongside the large banner, or the *carrosse*, of the city.

The city, in short, was the union of the neighbourhoods, streets, parishes and guilds, and had its plenary assembly in the grand forum, its grand belfry,[7] its elected judges, its banner to rally the militias of the guilds and neighbourhoods. It dealt with other cities as sovereign, federated with whom it wished, concluded alliances nationwide or even outwith its own nation. Thus, the English 'Cinque Ports' around Dover were federated with French and Dutch ports on the other side of the Channel;[8] the Russian Novgorod was the ally of the Germanic-Scandinavian Hansa and so on. In its external relations each city possessed all the attributes of the modern State and from that period was constituted, by free contracts, what was later known as international law, placed under the sanction of the public opinion of all the cities, and later more often violated than respected by States.

How often would a city, unable 'to find the sentence' in a particularly complicated case, send someone to 'seek the sentence' in a neighbouring city! How many times did the

---

7   In the cities of the Middle Ages the belfry was the symbol of communal freedoms obtained from the local feudal lord. As well as housing the bell which called the people to communal deliberations or to signal the approach of an enemy, it also held the communal charters that confirmed in writing the commune's freedoms (and the commitment of the local lord to respect them). (Editor)

8   The Confederation of Cinque Ports was a series of coastal towns in Kent and Sussex (Hastings, New Romney, Hythe, Dover, Sandwich) originally formed for military and trade purposes. The name is Norman French, meaning 'five ports'. (Editor)

prevailing spirit of that period—arbitration, rather than the authority of the judge—express itself by two communes taking a third as arbitrator!

The crafts did the same. They handled their commercial and craft arrangements independently of their cities and made their treaties without regard of nationality. And when, in our ignorance, we boast of our international congresses of workers, we forget that in the fifteenth century international congresses of crafts, even of apprentices, were already being held.

Lastly, the city either defended itself against aggressors and itself waged fierce wars against the feudal lords in the vicinity by naming each year one or rather two military commanders for its militias; or it accepted a 'military defender'—a prince or a duke which it selected for one year and dismissed at will. For the maintenance of his soldiers, he would generally be given the proceeds from judicial fines; but he was forbidden to interfere in the affairs of the city.[9]

Or else, too weak to free itself entirely from its neighbours the feudal vultures, it kept as a more or less permanent military defender its bishop or a particular prince—Guelph or Ghibelline in Italy, the Rurik family in Russia, or Algirdas in Lithuania—but was jealously vigilant in preventing the authority of the bishop or the prince extending beyond the men encamped in the castle. It even forbade him to enter the town without permission. To this day the King of England cannot enter the City of London without the permission of its Lord Mayor.

The economic life of the cities in the Middle Ages deserves to be recounted in detail but I am forced to overlook it here and refer the reader to what I have said in *Mutual Aid* basing myself on a vast body of modern historical research. It will suffice to simply note that internal commerce was always dealt with by the guilds—not by individual artisans—prices being set by mutual agreement. Furthermore, at the beginning of

---

9   In Russia, we know of hundreds of these annual contracts concluded between the cities (their *vétche*, or *forum*) and princes.

this period external commerce was dealt with *exclusively by the city*. Only later did it become the monopoly of the Merchants' Guild and, later still, of isolated individuals. Finally, they never worked on Sunday, nor on Saturday afternoon (bath day). The supply of the main staples was always handled by the city, and this custom was preserved for wheat in some Swiss towns until the middle of the nineteenth century.

In short it is shown by a huge mass of documents of all kinds that humanity has never known, neither before nor after, a period of relative well-being equally assured to all as existed in the cities of the Middle Ages. The present poverty, insecurity and overwork were unknown.

V

With these elements—freedom, organisation from the simple to the complex, production and exchange by the crafts (guilds), foreign trade handled by the whole city and not by individuals and the purchase of provisions by the city to supply them to the citizens at cost price—with these elements the towns of the Middle Ages during the first two centuries of their free existence became centres of well-being for all the inhabitants, centres of opulence and civilisation, as has never been seen since.

We have but to consult the documents which enable us to establish the rate of remuneration for labour compared to the cost of commodities—[Thorold] Rogers[10] has done this for England and a great number of German writers for Germany—and we see that the labour of the artisan and even of a simple day-labourer was at that time remunerated at a rate that is not reached in our time, not even by the working-class elite.

---

10 James Edwin Thorold Rogers (1823–1890) was an English economist, historian and Liberal politician whose works include *Six Centuries of Work and Wages: The History of English Labour* (1884) and *The Economic Interpretation of History* (1888). (Editor)

The account books of the colleges of the University of Oxford (which have been kept for seven centuries since the twelfth century) and of certain English estates, [as well as] those of a large number of German and Swiss towns, are there to bear witness.

When we consider, in addition, the artistic finish and the amount of decorative work the worker then put equally into the beautiful works of art he produced and into the simplest items of domestic life—a gate, a candlestick, a piece of pottery—and we see that during his work he did not know the rush, the over-work of our time; that he could forge, sculpt, weave, embroider with leisure—as only a very small number of worker-artists amongst us can do today.

And let us finally browse through the donations made to the churches and the communal houses of the parish, the guild or the city, whether in works of art—in decorative panels, sculptures, wrought or cast metal—or in money, and we realise the degree of well-being these cities were able to achieve; we can also sense the spirit of research and invention which pre-vailed there, the air of freedom which inspired their works, the feeling of fraternal solidarity which was established in these guilds, where men of the same trade were linked not merely by the commercial and technical side of the trade but by ties of sociability, of brotherhood. Was it not, in fact, the law of the guild that two brothers had to attend the bedside of each sick brother—a custom which certainly required devotion in those times of contagious diseases and plagues—to follow him to the grave, to take care of his widow and children?

The abject poverty, the debasement, the uncertain future for the many and the isolation of poverty which characterise our modern cities were absolutely unknown in those 'free oases, arising in the twelfth century amidst the feudal forest'.

In those cities, sheltered by the conquered liberties, under the impetus of the spirit of free agreement and of free initiative, a whole new civilisation grew up and reached such a blossoming that we have not seen its like in history to the present day.

All modern industry comes to us from these cities. In three centuries, industries and the arts reached such perfection that our century has only been able to surpass them in speed of production but rarely in quality and very rarely in the beauty of the product. All the arts we seek in vain to revive now—the beauty of Raphael, the strength and boldness of Michelangelo, the art and science of Leonardo da Vinci, the poetry and language of Dante, the architecture, finally, to which we owe the cathedrals of Laon, Rheims, Cologne, Pisa, Florence—as Victor Hugo so well put it 'the people was the builder'[11]—the treasures of the beauty of Florence and Venice, the town halls of Bremen and Prague, the towers of Nuremberg and Pisa and so on *ad infinitum*—all this was the product of that period.

Do you wish to measure the progress of that civilisation at a glance? Compare the dome of St. Mark in Venice with the rustic arch of the Normans; the paintings of Raphael with the embroidery of the Bayeux Tapestries; the mathematical and physics instruments and the clocks of Nuremberg with the hourglasses of the preceding centuries; the rich language of Dante with the barbaric Latin of the tenth century. A new world was born between the two!

Never, with the exception of that other glorious period— again of free cities—of ancient Greece, had humanity made such a leap forward. Never, in two or three centuries, had man undergone a change so profound nor so extended his power over the forces of nature.

Perhaps you are thinking of the civilisation of our century whose progress we are constantly praising? But in each of its

---

11   A slight paraphrase ('le peuple en fut le maçon') of Victor Hugo's 1831
     novel *Notre-Dame de Paris* (translated as *The Hunchback of Notre-Dame*):
     'Le temps est l'architecte, le peuple est le maçon'. ('The time is the
     architect, the people is the builder'.) (Editor)

manifestations it is only the daughter of the civilisation that grew up within the free communes. All the great discoveries made by modern science—the compass, the clock, the watch, printing, maritime discoveries, gunpowder, the laws of gravitation, atmospheric pressure of which the steam engine was only a development, the rudiments of chemistry, the scientific method already indicated by Roger Bacon and practiced in Italian universities—where did all these come from if not the free cities, in the civilisation which was developed under the shelter of communal liberties?

But it may be said that I forget the conflicts, the internal struggles, with which the history of these communes is filled, the turmoil of the streets, the bitter battles against the lords, the insurrections of the 'young arts' against the 'old arts', the bloodshed and reprisals of these struggles.

Well, no, I forget nothing. But like Leo and Botta—the two historians of medieval Italy—like Sismondi, like Ferrari, Gino Capponi and so many others, I see that these struggles were the very guarantee of a free life in the free city. I perceive a renewal, a new impetus towards progress after each of those struggles. After having recounted in detail these struggles and conflicts and having also measured the immensity of the progress achieved while these struggles bloodied the streets—the well-being assured to all the inhabitants, the civilisation renewed—Leo and Botta concluded with this thought, [which is] so right, which often comes to my mind; I would like to see it engraved in the minds of every modern revolutionary: 'A commune', they said, 'only presents the image of a moral whole, is only universal in its manner of being, like the human mind itself, *only when it has admitted conflict, opposition*'.[12]

---

12   Kropotkin's emphasis, Henri Leo and Carlo Botta, *Histoire d'Italie, depuis les premiers temps jusqu'a nos jours*, vol. 1 (Paris: Béthune et Plon, 1844), 462. (Editor)

Yes, conflict, freely debated, without any external power, the State, coming to throw its immense weight into the balance in favour of one of the forces engaged in the struggle.

Like those two authors, I also believe that we have often caused 'much more evil by *imposing* peace, because we linked together opposites in wanting to create a general political order and sacrificed individualities and small organisms, in order to absorb them in a vast body without colour and without life'.[13]

That is why the communes—so long as they did not themselves seek to become States and to impose around them 'submission in a vast body without colour and without life'—that is why they grew and emerged rejuvenated from every struggle, flourishing with the clash of weapons in the streets; whereas two centuries later this same civilisation collapsed at the sound of wars fathered by States.

In the commune, struggle was for the conquest and upholding of the liberty of the individual, for the federative principle, for the right to unite and to act; whereas the wars of the States were intended to extinguish these liberties, to subjugate the individual, to annihilate free agreement, to unite men in the same servitude in relation to the king, the judge, the priest—the State.

Therein lies all the difference. There are struggles and conflicts that destroy. And there are those which hurl humanity forward.

---

13 This is a slight paraphrase of Henri Leo and Carlo Botta: 'more harm was done by peace through war, because we linked together opposites in seeking to create a general political order and sacrificed individualities and small ways of living [*les petits existences*], in order to absorb them in a vast body without colour and without life' (*Histoire d'Italie, depuis les premiers temps jusqu'a nos jours*, vol. 1 [Paris: Béthune et Plon, 1844], 751). (Editor)

VI

During the course of the sixteenth century the modern barbarians destroyed all this civilisation of the cities of the Middle Ages. These barbarians did not succeed in annihilating it, but they succeeded in halting its progress for at least two or three centuries. They threw it in a new direction, in which humanity struggles with difficulty at the moment, not knowing how to escape.

They subjugated the individual. They stripped him of all his liberties and required him to forget all his associations based on free agreement and free initiative. Their aim was to level the whole of society to an identical submission to the master. They destroyed all ties between men, declaring that the State and the Church alone must henceforth form the association between their subjects; that the Church and the State alone have the task of watching over the industrial, commercial, judicial, artistic and personal interests for which men of the twelfth century were accustomed to unite directly.

And who are these barbarians? It is the State: the triple alliance, finally constituted, of the military chief, the Roman judge, and the priest—the three forming a mutual insurance for domination—the three, united in one power which will command in the name of the interests of society—and will crush that society.

We ask ourselves, naturally, how were these new barbarians able to overcome the communes, once so powerful? Where did they find the strength for conquest?

They found this force, first of all, in the village. Just as the communes of ancient Greece were unable to abolish slavery and perished because of that—so the communes of the Middle Ages did not know how to free the peasant from serfdom along with the town dweller.

It is true that almost everywhere the town dweller—an artisan-farmer himself—had at the time of his emancipation sought to rouse the countryside to help him gain their freedom. For two centuries, the townspeople in Italy, Spain and Germany had sustained a bitter war against the feudal lords. Feats of heroism and perseverance were displayed by the burghers in this war on the castles. They bled themselves white to become masters of the castles of feudalism and to fell the feudal forest that surrounded them.

But they were only partially successful. War-weary, they finally made peace over the heads of the peasant. To buy peace, they handed him over to the lord as long as he lived outside the territory conquered by the commune. In Italy and Germany they ended up accepting the lord as fellow burgher, on condition that he came to live in the commune. Elsewhere, they ended by sharing his domination over the peasant. And the lord took his revenge on the 'low people' of the towns, whom he hated and despised, bathing the streets in blood by conflicts and the practice of retaliation of the noble families, who did not bring their differences before the syndics and the communal judges but settled them by the sword in the street, hurling one part of community against another.

The lord also demoralised the commune with his largesse, his intrigues, his lordly way of life and by his education received at the court of the bishop or the king. He convinced it to embrace his struggles. And the burgher ended by imitating the lord: he became lord in his turn, also enriching himself by distant commerce or from the labour of the serfs confined in the villages.

After which the peasant gave the emerging kings, emperors, tsars and the popes his assistance when they began building their kingdoms and subjecting the towns. Where the peasant did not march under their orders, he did not oppose them.

It is in the countryside, in a fortified castle situated in the middle of rural communities that royalty was slowly established. In the twelfth century, it existed in name only, and we know today what to think of the bandits, chiefs of small bands of brigands, who adorned themselves with that name: a name which—as Augustin Thierry has so well demonstrated—did not mean very much at the time, when there were 'the king (the superior, the senior) of the basoche',[14] 'the king of the nets' (amongst fishermen), 'the king of the beggars'.

Slowly, gropingly, a baron better placed in a region, more powerful or more cunning than the others, succeeded, here and there, in raising himself above his fellows. The Church hastened to support him. And by force, guile, money, sword and poison if need be, one of these feudal barons grew [in power] at the expense of the others. But royal authority never succeeded in constituting itself in any of the free cities, which had their noisy forum, their Tarpeian Rock[15] or their river for the tyrants: it arose in the towns which had grown in the heart of the countryside.

After having sought in vain to establish this authority in Rheims, or in Laon, it was in Paris—an agglomeration of villages and boroughs surrounded by a rich countryside which had not yet known the life of free cities; it was in Westminster, at the gates of the populous City of London; it was in the Kremlin, built in the centre of rich villages on the banks of the Moskva [River], after having failed in Suzdal and in Vladimir—but never in Novgorod, Pskov, Nuremberg, Laon, or Florence—that royal authority was consolidated.

The peasants of the surrounding area supplied the emerging monarchies with food, horses and men, and commerce—royal

---

14 The *basoche* was the guild of the legal clerks of the court system from the Middle Ages until the French Revolution. The word derives from the Latin *basilica*, the kind of building in which the legal trade was practiced in the Middle Ages. (Editor)

15 The Tarpeian Rock was a steep cliff of the southern summit of the Capitoline Hill, overlooking the Roman Forum in Ancient Rome. It was used during the Roman Republic as an execution site for murderers, traitors, etc. (Editor)

and not communal in this case—increased their wealth. The Church swaddled them with its care. It protected them, came to their aid with its coffers, invented the local saint and his miracles for them. It enveloped with its worship Notre Dame of Paris or the image of the Virgin of Iberia in Moscow.[16] And while the civilisation of the free cities, freed from the bishops, seized its youthful elan, the Church worked hard to reconstitute its authority by means of the rising royalty, swaddled by its care, its incense and its coins, the royal cradle of the one it had finally chosen to rebuild with him, through him, its ecclesiastical authority. In Paris, Moscow, Madrid and Prague you see it leaning over the cradle of royalty, a lighted torch in its hand, the executioner by its side.

Fierce in its work, strong in its statist education, leaning on the man of will or cunning it took from any class of society, made for intrigue and versed in Roman and Byzantine law—you can see it relentlessly marching towards its ideal: the Hebrew king, absolute but obedient to the high priest—the secular arm at the orders of the ecclesiastical power.

In the sixteenth century this slow labour of the two conspirators is already in full force. A king already dominates the other barons, his rivals, and this power will soon fall upon the free cities to crush them in their turn.

Besides, the towns of the sixteenth century were no longer what they had been in the twelfth, thirteenth and fourteenth centuries.

---

16 The Panagia Portaitissa is an Eastern Orthodox icon of the Virgin Mary, which, according to the Sacred Tradition of the Eastern Orthodox Church, was painted by Luke the Evangelist and to which numerous miracles have been attributed. In 1648, Patriarch Nikon of Moscow, while he was still archimandrite of Novospassky Monastery, commissioned an exact copy of it to be made and sent to Russia. Almost immediately upon its arrival, the icon had numerous miracles attributed to it by the faithful. The Iverskaya Chapel was built in 1669 to enshrine the icon next to the Kremlin walls in Moscow. (Editor)

Born of the libertarian revolution, they did not have the courage or the strength to spread their ideas of equality to the neighbouring countryside, not even to those who had later settled within their walls, [those] sanctuaries of freedom, to create industrial crafts there.

In every town is found a distinction between the old families who had made the revolution of the twelfth century, or simply 'the families', and those who were established later in the city. The old 'merchant guild' would not hear of accepting the newcomers. It refused to incorporate the 'young arts' for [the purposes of] commerce. And, from the simple steward of the city that it once was when it carried out external trade for the whole city, it became the middleman who enriches itself on its own behalf through distant commerce. It imported Eastern ostentation, it became moneylender to the city and, later, joins with the burgher-lord and the priest against the 'lower classes'; or else it sought support from the emerging king to maintain its right to enrichment, its commercial monopoly. Becoming personal, commerce destroys the free city.

The guilds of the old crafts which at the beginning formed the city and its government also did not wish to recognise the same rights to the young guilds, established later by new crafts. These must conquer their rights by a revolution. And that is what they do everywhere. But if in certain cities this revolution becomes the starting point for a renewal of all the ways of life and all the arts (this is so clearly seen in Florence), in other cities it ends in the victory of the *popolo grasso* over the *popolo basso*[17]—by a crushing [of the rebellion], by mass deportations, by executions, especially when the lords and priests interfere.

And, needless to say, the king will use as a pretext the defence of the 'lower people' in order to crush the 'fat people'

17   Italian for 'common people' and 'fat people', respectively: during the
      Middle Ages in Italy, the wealthy and influential members of society
      were called *Popolo Grosse*, which literally meant 'fat people'. (Editor)

and to subjugate them both after he has made himself master of the city!

And then the cities had to die since *even men's ideas had changed*. The teaching of canon law and Roman law had modified the mind-set [of the people].

The European of the twelfth century was fundamentally a federalist. As a man of free initiative, of free agreement, of desired and freely entered associations, he saw in himself the point of departure for the whole of society. He did not seek safety through obedience nor did he ask for a saviour for society. The idea of Christian and Roman discipline was unknown to him.

But under the influence of the Christian Church—always in love with authority, always longing to impose its dominion over the souls and above all the labour of the faithful; and on the other hand, under the influence of Roman law, which, from the twelfth century onwards, had already appeared at the courts of powerful lords, kings and popes and soon became the favourite [subject of] study in the universities—under the influence of these two teachings which are so much in accord, though originally bitter enemies, minds became corrupted as the priest and the jurist triumphed.

Man fell in love with authority. A revolution of the lower crafts is accomplished in a commune, the commune calls for a saviour. It gives itself a dictator, a municipal Caesar; it grants him full powers to exterminate the opposition party. And he takes advantage of this, using all the refinements in cruelty suggested to him by the Church or by examples borrowed from the despotic kingdoms of the East.

The Church without doubt supports him. Had it not always dreamt of the biblical king who will kneel before the high priest and be his docile instrument? Has it not always hated with all its might those ideas of rationalism which breathed in the free towns during the first Renaissance, that of the twelfth century?

Did it not curse those 'pagan' ideas which brought man back to nature under the influence of the rediscovery of Greek civilisation? And, later, did it not get the princes to stifle these ideas which, in the name of primitive Christianity, raised men against the pope, the priest and religion in general? Fire, the [breaking] wheel and the gallows—those weapons so dear at all times to the Church—were used against the heretics. Whatever the instrument: pope, king or dictator—it matters little to it as long as fire, the wheel and the gallows operate against its enemies.

And under this double teaching of the Roman jurist and the priest, the federalist spirit which had made the free commune, the spirit of initiative and free agreement was dying to make way for the spirit of discipline, for pyramidal authoritarian organisation. Both the rich and the commoners demanded a saviour.

And when the saviour appeared; when the king, enriched far from the turmoil of the forum in some town of his creation, supported by the wealthy Church and followed by conquered nobles and their peasants, knocked at the gates of the cities, promising the 'lower classes' his lofty protection against the rich and the submissive rich his protection against the rebellious poor—the towns, already gnawed away by the blight of authority, lacked the strength to resist him.

The great invasions of Europe by waves of peoples once more coming from the East aided the rising royalty in this work of the concentration of powers.

The Mongols had conquered and devastated Eastern Europe in the thirteenth century, and soon an empire was founded there, in Moscow, under the protection of the Tartar khans and the Russian Christian Church. The Turks had come to settle in Europe and pushed as far as Vienna, devastating everything in their path. Thereupon, powerful States were formed in Poland, Bohemia, Hungary, in Central Europe, to resist these two invasions. While at the other end [of Europe], the war of extermination waged against the Moors in Spain allowed another powerful empire to constitute itself in Castile and Aragon, supported by the Roman Church and the Inquisition— by the sword and the stake.

These invasions and wars inevitably led Europe to enter a new phase—that of military States.

Since the communes themselves were becoming small States, these little States inevitably had to be swallowed up by the large ones.

VII

The victory of the State over the communes of the Middle Ages and the federalist institutions of the time was nevertheless not immediate. There was a period when it was threatened to the point of being in doubt.

An immense popular movement—religious in its form and expressions but eminently egalitarian and Communist in its aspirations—arose in the towns and countryside of Central Europe.

Already, in the fourteenth century (in 1358 in France and in 1381 in England), two similar great movements had taken place. The two powerful uprisings of the Jacquerie and of Wat Tyler had shaken society to its very foundations. Both, though, had been principally directed against the nobles and, though both had been defeated, they had broken feudal power. The uprising of peasants in England had put an end to serfdom and the Jacquerie in France had so severely checked serfdom in its development that henceforth the institution simply vegetated, without ever reaching the power that it was to achieve later in Germany and Eastern Europe.

Now, in the sixteenth century, a similar movement took place in Central Europe. Under the name of the Hussite uprising in Bohemia, Anabaptism in Germany, Switzerland and in the Low Countries, it was—besides the revolt against the lord—a comprehensive revolt against the State and Church, against Roman and canon law, in the name of primitive Christianity.[18]

Long misrepresented by statist and ecclesiastical historians, this movement is just beginning to be understood today.

The absolute freedom of the individual, who must only obey the commands of his conscience, and Communism were the watchwords of this uprising. And it was only later, after the State and Church had succeeded in exterminating its most ardent champions and misappropriated it for their own benefit, that this movement, diminished [in scope] and deprived of its revolutionary character, became the Lutheran Reformation.

With Luther the movement was welcomed by the princes; but it had begun as Communist Anarchism, preached and put into practice in some places. And if we disregard the religious phrasing which was a tribute to the times, we find in it the very essence of the current of ideas which we represent today: the negation of laws—laws of the State or allegedly divine [in origin]—the conscience of the individual being his one and only law; the commune, absolute master of its destiny, taking back from the lords communal lands and refusing any personal or money fee to the State;[19] Communism in a word, and equality put into practice. So when Denck, one of the philosophers of the Anabaptist movement, was asked if he nevertheless did not acknowledge the authority of the Bible, he replied that the only rule of conduct which each individual finds *for himself* in the Bible was obligatory for him. And yet these same, so vague,

---

18 The 'times of troubles' in Russia at the beginning of the seventeenth century represent a similar movement directed against serfdom and the State but without a religious basis.

19 Medieval serfs did not receive land as a free gift. To use it they owed certain duties to their lord. These took the form of personal services (such as working on the lord's fields for two or three days each week) or paying a fee for certain activities (for example, being obliged to use the lord's mill to grind their wheat). They were also expected to provide personal services in labour, as well as taxes to the monarchy. (Editor)

phrases—derived from ecclesiastical jargon—this authority of 'the book', from which is so easily borrowed arguments for and against Communism, for and against authority, and so undecided when it is a question of clearly affirming freedom—did not this religious tendency already contain the seeds of the certain defeat of the uprising?

Born in the towns, the movement soon spread to the countryside. The peasants refused to obey anybody and, fixing an old shoe on a pike by way of a flag, reclaimed the land from the lords, broke the bonds of serfdom, drove away the priests and judges, and formed themselves into free communes. And it was only by the stake, the wheel and the gallows, it was only by massacring more than a hundred thousand peasants in a few years that royal or imperial power, allied with that of the papal or the Reformed Church—Luther encouraging the massacre of the peasants even more vehemently than the Pope—put an end to those uprisings which had threatened for a time the formation of the emerging States.

Born from popular Anabaptism, the Lutheran Reformation, supported by the State, massacred the people and crushed the movement from which it had drawn its strength at its origin. Then the remnants of the popular wave sought refuge in the communities of the 'Moravian Brothers', who, in turn, were destroyed a century later by the Church and the State. Those of them who were not exterminated sought sanctuary, some in south-eastern Russia (the Mennonite community that has since emigrated to Canada) and others to Greenland where they could continue to live to this day in communities refusing all service to the State.

Henceforth the State was assured of its existence. The jurist, the priest and the warlord, constituted in a joint alliance around the thrones, could pursue their work of annihilation.

What lies, amassed by statist historians in the pay of the State, on that period!

Indeed, have we not all learned at school for instance that the State rendered the great service of forming, on the ruins of feudal society, the national unions previously made impossible by the rivalries between cities? Having learned this at school, almost all of us have continued to believe this into middle age.

And yet we learn today that in spite of all the rivalries the medieval cities had already worked for four centuries to establish these unions by desired, freely agreed federation and had succeeded.

The Lombardy union, for example, encompassed the cities of Northern Italy, with its federal treasury in Milan. Other federations such as the Tuscany union, the Rhineland union (which included sixty towns), the federations of Westphalia, of Bohemia, of Serbia, of Poland, of Russian towns covered Europe. At the same time, the commercial union of the Hanse included Scandinavian, German, Polish and Russian towns throughout the Baltic basin. There were already all the elements as well as the fact itself of freely formed large human agglomerations.

Do you want the living proof of these groupings? You have it in Switzerland! There the union initially asserted itself between the village communes (the old cantons), just as it was formed in France at the same time in Laon. And since in Switzerland the separation between town and village had not been as deep as [in those places] where the towns were engaged in large-scale distant commerce, the towns gave assistance to the peasant insurrection of the sixteenth century and then the union included towns and villages to constitute a federation which continues to this day.

But the State, by its very nature, cannot tolerate free federation: it represents that horror of all jurists, 'a State within the State'. The State does not recognise a freely agreed union operating within it; it knows only *subjects*. Only it and its sister, the Church, arrogate the right to serve as the link between men.

Consequently, the State must inevitably destroy cities based on the direct union between citizens. It must abolish all association within the city, abolish the city itself, and destroy all direct association between the cities. For the federal principle it must substitute the principle of submission, of discipline. That is its essence. Without this principle it ceases to be a State.

And the sixteenth century—a century of carnage and wars—is fully summed up by this struggle of the rising State against the free towns and their federations. The towns were besieged, stormed, sacked, their inhabitants decimated or deported.

The State eventually wins total victory. And these are the consequences:

In the sixteenth century Europe was covered with rich cities, whose artisans, masons, weavers and engravers produced marvels of art; their universities laid the foundations of modern empirical science, their caravans roamed the continents, their vessels ploughed the rivers and seas.

What remained two centuries later? Towns that had as many as fifty to a hundred thousand inhabitants and which had possessed (as was the case in Florence) more schools and in the communal hospitals more beds per person than there are now possessed in the towns best equipped in this respect became rotten boroughs.[20] Their populations massacred or deported, the State and Church seized their wealth. Industry dies under the strict supervision of the employees of the State. Commerce is dead. Even the roads which had once linked these cities together became impassable in the seventeenth century.

---

20 The term *rotten borough* came into use in eighteenth century Britain and signified a parliamentary borough with a tiny electorate. This meant that the electorate could not vote as they pleased due to dependency on and pressure by the local landlord, when the electorate was not reduced to just him. Usually these boroughs were once more populous and important and so the word 'rotten' had the connotation of corruption as well as that of long-term decline. (Editor)

The State is war. And wars devastated Europe, completing the ruin of the towns which the State had not yet directly destroyed.

The towns crushed, at least the villages gained something from the concentration of State control? Of course not! Read what the historians tell us of life in the countryside in Scotland, in Tuscany, in Germany during the sixteenth century and compare their accounts with those of the misery in England in the years before 1648, in France under the 'Sun King', Louis XIV, in Germany, in Italy, everywhere, after a century of statist domination.

Misery—everywhere. All are unanimous in recognising it, in reporting it. Where serfdom had been abolished, it is reconstituted under a thousand new forms; and where it had not yet been destroyed, it was shaped under the protection of the State into a savage institution bearing all the characteristics of ancient slavery or worse. In Russia it was the rising State of the Romanovs that introduced serfdom and soon gave it the form of slavery.

But could anything else come out of statist misery, since its first concern, after [crushing] the towns, was to annihilate the village commune, destroy all the ties that existed between the peasants, to deliver their lands to plundering by the rich, to subjugate them, every individual, to the functionary, the priest, the lord?

VIII

To annihilate the independence of the cities; to pillage the rich guilds of merchants and artisans; to centralise in its hands the external commerce of the cities and ruin it; to seize the internal administration of the guilds and subject internal commerce as well as the manufacture of anything, down to the smallest detail, to [the control of] a host of functionaries—and in this way kill industry and the crafts; to seize the local militias and the whole of the municipal administration, to crush the weak for the benefit of the strong by taxation, and ruining countries by wars—such was the role of the emerging State in the sixteenth and seventeenth centuries in relation to urban agglomerates.

The same tactic [was used], obviously, for the villages, for the peasants. As soon as the State felt strong enough, it hastened to destroy the commune in the village, to ruin the peasants in its clutches and to plunder the common lands.

Historians and economists in the pay of the State teach us, of course, that the village commune having become an outdated form of land possession—a form which hindered the progress of agriculture—had to disappear under 'the action of natural economic forces'. The bourgeois politicians and economists keep repeating this to the present day; and there are even revolutionaries and Socialists—those who claim to be scientific—who recite this commonplace fable, taught at school.

Well, never has a more odious lie been asserted in science. A conscious lie, for history abounds with documents to prove for those who want to know—for France, it would almost be enough to [just] consult Dalloz—that the village commune was initially deprived of all its powers by the State; its independence, its juridical and legislative powers; and then its lands were either simply stolen by the rich under the protection of the State or directly confiscated by the State.

In France the pillage started as early as the sixteenth century and followed its course at a faster pace in the following century. From 1659, the State took the communes under its lofty tutelage, and we have only to consult Louis XIV's edict of 1667 to discover the scale of the plunder of communal properties at that time.[21] 'Each has put up with it according to his propriety . . . they have divided them . . . to strip the communes

---

21 Edit du Roi, portant règlement général sur les Communes et Communaux des Paroisses et Communautés d'Habitants, April 1667;

they used fictitious debts', said the 'Sun King' in that edict . . .
and two years later he confiscated all the income of the communes for his own benefit. This is called a 'natural death' in
the language which claims to be scientific.

In the following century, it is estimated that half, at least,
of communal land was simply appropriated by the nobility
and the clergy under the patronage of the State. And yet the
commune continued to exist until 1787. The village assembly
gathered under the elm [tree], apportioned the lands, distributed the [demands for] taxes—you can find the evidence in
Babeau (*Le village sous l'ancien régime* [The Village Under the
Ancien Régime]). Turgot, in the province in which he was the
Intendant,[22] had already found the village assemblies 'too noisy'
and under his administration they were abolished, replaced by
assemblies elected from amongst the village bigwigs. And on
the eve of the Revolution, in 1787, the State generalised that
measure. The *mir* was abolished and the affairs of the commune
thus fell into the hands of a few syndics elected by the richest
bourgeois and peasants.

The Constituent Assembly was quick in confirming this
law, in December 1789, and the bourgeois then replaced the
lords in stripping the communes of what remained of their
communal lands. It then needed Jacquerie after Jacquerie to
force the Convention, in 1793, to confirm what the rebellious
peasants had just achieved in eastern France. That is to say,
the Convention ordered the return of the communal lands to
the peasants—something which, moreover, only took place
where it was already achieved by revolutionary action. It is time to
understand that this is the fate of all revolutionary laws. They
only come into effect when the fact is already accomplished.

---

see Le Gras de Gallon, *Conférence de l'ordonnance de Louis XIV du mois d'août
1669, sur le fait des Euaux et Forests*, vol. 2 (Paris, 1725), 258–61. (Editor)

22 An intendant was a royal civil servant in the pre-revolution monarchy
and was considered a symbol of royal centralisation and absolutism.
Turgot was the intendant of Limoges between 1761 and 1774. (Editor)

But while recognising the right of the communes to the lands that had been taken away from them since 1669, the law had to add its bourgeois venom. Its intention was that the communal lands should be divided in equal parts only between 'citizens'—that is to say amongst the village bourgeoisie.[23] By a stroke of the pen it wanted to dispossess the 'inhabitants' and the mass of the impoverished peasants, who were most in need of these lands. Thereupon, fortunately, there were new Jacqueries, and in July 1793 the Convention authorised the division of the land by head between all the inhabitants—something, again, which was only done here and there, but which served as a pretext for a new pillage of communal lands.[24]

Were these measures not already enough to cause what these gentlemen call 'the natural death' of the commune? And yet the commune still lived. Then, on 24 August 1794, the reaction coming to power struck the major blow. The State confiscated all the lands of the communes and used them as a fund to guarantee the national debt, putting them up for auction and delivering them to its creatures, the Thermidorians.

On the 2 Prairial Year V,[25] after three years of scrambling [for the spoils], this law was happily repealed. But, at the same time, the communes were abolished and replaced by cantonal councils, so that the State could more easily pack them with its creatures. This lasted until 1801 when the village communes were reintroduced; but then the government itself undertook to appoint the mayors and syndics in each of the

---

23 Kropotkin discusses the desire by the bourgeois to limit political involvement to 'active' citizens (defined by having a certain amount of wealth) and exclude 'passive' citizens (that is, the working classes) in chapter LIX of *The Great French Revolution* (Montréal: Black Rose Books, 1989). (Editor)

24 Kropotkin discusses the fate of the communal lands in chapters XLVIII and XLIX of *The Great French Revolution*. (Editor)

25 Kropotkin is using the French Revolutionary Calendar for 21 May 1797. (Editor)

thirty-six thousand communes! And this absurdity lasted until the Revolution of July 1830; after which the law of 1789 was reintroduced. And, in the meantime, the communal lands were again confiscated entirely by the State in 1813 and pillaged anew for three years. What remained was not returned to the communes until 1816.

Do you think that was the end? Not at all! Each new regime saw in the communal lands a means of rewarding its hench-men. Thus, from 1830, on three different occasions—the first in 1837 and the last under Napoleon III—laws were enacted to *force* the peasants to divide what remained of their communal forests and pastures, and three times the State was obliged to annul those laws on account of the resistance of the peasants. All the same, Napoleon III took advantage of it to seize a few large estates and to make presents of them to his creatures.

Such are the facts. And this is what these gentlemen call, in 'scientific' language, the natural death of communal owner-ship 'under the influence of economic laws'. We might as well call the massacre of a hundred thousand soldiers on the bat-tlefield a natural death!

Well, what was done in France was done in Belgium, in England, in Germany, in Austria—everywhere in Europe, except in the Slav countries.[26]

But no matter! The periods of increased pillaging of the communes are similar throughout Western Europe. Only the methods vary. Thus, in England they did not dare to proceed by general measures; they preferred to pass through Parliament some thousands of separate Enclosure Acts (acts of 'demarca-tion') by which, in every particular case, Parliament sanctioned the confiscation—*it does so to this day*—and gave the lord the right to keep the communal lands that he had enclosed by a fence. And while nature had hitherto followed the narrow

---

26 It is already being done in Russia, the government having authorised the pillaging of communal lands by the law of 1906 and encouraged this pillage through its functionaries.

furrows by which the communal fields were temporarily divided between the various families of a village in England, and that we have in the works of a certain Marshall clear descriptions of this form of possession at the beginning of the nineteenth century,[27] while the communal household was still retained in some municipalities up to the present,[28] there is no lack of scholars (such as Seebohm, worthy emulator of Fustel de Coulanges) to maintain and teach that the commune never existed in England as anything other than a form of serfdom!

In Belgium, in Germany, in Italy, in Spain we find the same methods [at work]. And, in one way or another, the individual appropriation of the formally communal lands was almost completed in Western Europe by the fifties of the nineteenth century. The peasants have retained only scraps of their communal lands.

This is the way that this mutual insurance between the lord, the priest, the soldier and the judge which has the name 'the State' behaved towards the peasants, in order to strip them of their last guarantee against destitution and economic servitude.

But while it was approving and organising this pillage, could the State respect the institution of the commune as an organ of local life?

Obviously not.

To admit that citizens could constitute between themselves a federation which appropriates some of the functions of the State would have been a contradiction in principle. The

---

27 'Marshall's works, which passed unnoticed until Nasse and Sir Henry Maine drew attention to them, leave no doubt as to the village community system having been widely spread, in nearly all English counties, at the beginning of the nineteenth century'; Kropotkin, *Mutual Aid: A factor of Evolution* (London: Freedom Press, 2009), 190. (Editor)

28 See Dr. Gilbert Slater, 'The Inclosure of Common Fields', in the *Geographical Journal* of the Geographical Society of London, with plans and maps, January 1907. Later published in volume form.

State demands from its subjects direct personal submission without intermediaries; it wants equality in servitude; it cannot allow 'the State within the State'.

Also, as soon as the State began to form itself in the sixteenth century, it worked to destroy all the ties of association which existed between citizens, whether in the town or the village. If it tolerated, under the name of municipal institutions, some remnants of autonomy—never of independence—it was only for a fiscal purpose, to correspondingly reduce the central budget; or else, to enable the bigwigs of the province to get rich at the expense of the people, as was the case in England, [quite] legally until recent years, and in institutions and customs to this day.

This is understandable. Local life is [based on] customary right, whereas the centralisation of powers is [a matter of] Roman law. The two cannot live side by side; one must destroy the other.

That is why under the French regime in Algeria when a Kabyle *djemmah*—a village commune—wants to plead for its lands, each inhabitant of the commune must lodge a separate complaint with the courts, which will judge fifty or two hundred separate cases rather than accept the collective complaint of the commune. The Jacobin code developed in the Code Napoleon hardly knows customary law: it prefers Roman law, or rather Byzantine law.

That is why, still in France, when the wind blows down a tree onto the national road or a peasant who does not want to do the *corvée* labour[29] himself to repair a communal road prefers to pay two or three francs to a stone breaker [to do it]—it is

---

29   A form of unpaid, unfree labour usually associated with medieval and early modern Europe. It was owed by a serf to their feudal lord or to royalty. When imposed by a State for the purposes of public works, it was termed statue labour. It was usually intermittent in nature and for limited periods of time—such as a certain number of days' work a year. (Editor)

necessary that twelve to fifteen employees of the Ministries of the Interior and of Finance be set into motion and that *more than fifty documents* pass between these austere functionaries before the tree can be sold or before the peasant receives permission to pay two or three francs to the municipal treasury.

You doubt it, perhaps? Well, you will find these fifty documents, listed and duly numbered by M. Tricoche, in the *Journal des Economistes* (April 1893).

That was, of course, under the Third Republic, for I do not speak of the barbaric procedures of the Ancien Régime which was satisfied with five or at the most six documents. Also, the scholars will tell you that in this barbaric time, control by the State was a sham.

And if it were only that! It would be, after all, only some twenty thousand functionaries too many, and another billion added to the budget. A mere trifle for the lovers of 'order' and alignment!

But there is worse at the bottom of all this. There is the *principle* that destroys everything.

The peasants of a village have a thousand common interests: interests of household, of neighbourhood, of continuous relationships. They are inevitably led to unite for a thousand different things. But the State does not want, cannot allow, that they are united! Since it gives them the school and the priest, the gendarme and the judge—that should be enough for them. And if other interests arise—they can be dealt with through the channels of State and Church!

Thus, until 1883, villagers in France were strictly prohibited from combining, if only for bulk-buying chemical fertilisers or irrigating of their meadows. It was not until 1883–1886 that the Republic decided to grant the peasants this right by voting in the law on trade unions, which was hedged in with strong provisos and restrictions.

And we, stupefied by State education, we rejoice in the sudden advances achieved by agricultural unions without blushing at the thought that this right which has been denied the peasants until now in the Middle Ages belonged without question to every man—free or serf. Slaves that we are, we already view this as a 'conquest for democracy'.

This is the state of stupefaction we have reached with our false education, tainted by the State and our Statist prejudices!

IX

'If you have common interests in the town and the village then ask the State and the Church to deal with them. But it is forbidden for you to combine directly to deal with them yourselves!' Such is the concept that echoes across Europe since the sixteenth century.

'All alliances and covines of masons and carpenters, and congregations, chapters, ordinances and oaths betwixt them made, or to be made, shall be from henceforth void and wholly annulled' reads an edict by Edward III, King of England, at the end of the fourteenth century.[30] But it was necessary to defeat

---

30 This Act of Edward III was issued in 1360 and continued as follows: 'so that every mason and carpenter, of what condition that he be, shall be compelled by his master to whom he serveth to do every work that to him pertaineth to do'. In addition, the *Ordinance of Labourers* imposed in 1349 was followed by the *Statue of Labourers* in 1351 (the latter was confirmed fifteen years later, in 1368). Both were ultimately vain attempts to aid landlords and masters facing labour shortages caused by the Black Death by freezing wages at the level they were before the plague by prohibiting increases in wages to a maximum (that paid in 1346), as well as the movement of workers from their home areas in search of better conditions: '[I]t was ordained by our lord king . . . against the malice of servants who were idle and not willing to serve after the pestilence without excessive wages, that such manner of servants, men as well as women, should be bound to serve, receiving the customary salary and wages in the places where they are bound to serve . . . and that the same servants refusing to serve in such a manner should be punished by imprisonment of their bodies . . . servants having no regard to the ordinance but to their ease and singular covetousness, do withdraw themselves from serving great men and others, unless

the towns and of the popular insurrections of which we have spoken for the State to dare to lay its hands on all the institutions—guilds, brotherhoods, etc.—which bound the artisans together and dissolve them, to destroy them.

This is what is seen so clearly in England, where we have a mass of documents [available] to follow this movement step by step. Little by little the State lays its hands on all the guilds and brotherhoods. It tights its grip on them, abolishes their conjurations, their syndics (which it replaces by its functionaries), their tribunals, their feasts; and at the beginning of the sixteenth century, under Henry VIII, the State confiscates without any kind of procedure all that the guilds possess. The heir of the great Protestant king completes his work.[31]

It is daylight robbery, without apologies, as Thorold Rogers said so well. And it is again this theft that the so-called

---

they have livery and wages double or treble of what they were wont ... to the great damage of the great men and impoverishment of all the commonality; whereof the commonality prays remedy. Wherefore in the parliament by the assent of the prelates, earls, barons, and those of the commonality assembled there, in order to refrain the malice of the servants' (*Statue of Labourers*).

They also mandated that all able-bodied men and women under sixty must work and imposed harsh penalties on those who remained idle. Both laws were very unpopular and were contributing factors to subsequent social unrest in England, most notably the Peasants' Revolt of 1381. (Editor)

31 A reference to an Act passed in the last year of the reign of Henry VIII seizing all the funds of the guilds (used for the welfare of its members and their families) and other properties. The confiscation of guild land (whose revenue was used to generate these funds and to provide interest-free loans) was planned by Henry VIII but carried out when his son Edward VI (1537–1553) assumed the throne in 1547. Henry's daughter, Elizabeth (1533–1603), continued the long sorry history of State action against labour by enacting the *Statute of Artificers* of 1563, which sought to fix prices, impose maximum wages and restrict workers' freedom of movement, as well as transferring to the newly forming English State functions previously held by the craft guilds. Local magistrates regulated wages, while workers required permission to move employers. The Statute was abolished in 1813. (Editor)

scientific economists represent as the 'natural' death of the guilds under the influence of 'economic laws'!

Indeed, could the State tolerate the guild, the trade corporation, with its tribunal, its militia, its treasury, its sworn organisation? It was 'the State within the State'! The real State *had* to destroy it and this it did everywhere: in England, in France, in Germany, in Bohemia and in Russia, retaining only the appearance as an instrument of the tax collector, as part of its vast administrative machine.

And—is it any wonder that the guilds, master craftsmen and *jurande*s,[32] deprived of all that hitherto had been their lives, placed under [the control of] royal functionaries, became mere cogs in the [machinery of] administration, that by the eighteenth century they were no more than an obstruction, a hindrance, to the development of industries, whereas previously they were life itself for four centuries. The State had killed them.

But it was not enough for the State to abolish all the workings of the inner life of the sworn brotherhoods of the crafts which hindered it by placing themselves between it and its subjects. It was not enough for it to confiscate their funds and their properties. It had to seize their functions, as well as their money.

In a city of the Middle Ages when there was a conflict of interests within a trade or two different guilds were in disagreement, there was no other recourse than the city. They had to come to an agreement, to arrive at some kind of compromise, since all were mutually bound together in the city. And this never failed to be done—by arbitration, by appeal to another city if need be.

Henceforth the State was the sole judge. At times all the local, insignificant disputes in small towns with a few hundred

---

32 The *jurande* was a guild body made up of its *juré*, members of the guild elected (usually for one year) to represent it and defend its interests. (Editor)

inhabitants were piled up in the form of documents in the offices of the king or of parliament. The English Parliament was literally inundated by thousands of these minor local squabbles. It then took thousands of functionaries in the capital—most of them corruptible—to read, classify, evaluate all these, to pronounce on the smallest detail: [for example] to regulate the manner in which a horseshoe had to be forged, how to bleach linen, to salt herrings, to make a barrel and so on ad infinitum, and the flood [of issues] always rose!

But this was not all. Before long the State laid its hands on the export trade. It saw a source of enrichment—and seized it. Formerly, when a dispute arose between two towns over the value of exported cloth or the quality of wool or the capacity of herring barrels, the towns themselves would remonstrate with each other. If the dispute dragged on, a third city was approached to judge it as arbitrator (this was constantly seen). Or else a congress of the guilds of the weavers or coopers was convened to resolve on an international level the quality and value of cloth or the capacity of barrels.

Henceforth it was the State in London or in Paris which undertook to settle all these disputes. Through its functionaries it regulated the capacity of barrels, defined the quality of cloth, specified and ordered the number of threads and their thickness in the warp and the weave, meddled by its ordinances with the smallest details of every industry.

You can guess with what result. Industry was dying in the eighteenth century under this supervision.

What had become, indeed, of the art of Benvenuto Cellini under the tutelage of the State? It disappeared! And the architecture of those guilds of masons and carpenters whose works of art we still admire? Just look at the hideous monuments of the statist period and at a glance you will judge that architecture was dead, so dead that it has not yet recovered from the blows dealt to it by the State.

What became of the textiles of Bruges, the cloth from Holland? Where were those blacksmiths, so skilled in handling iron and who, in every European town, knew how to make this thankless metal lend itself to [the creation of] the most exquisite designs? Where were those turners, those watchmakers, those fitters who had made Nuremberg one of the glories of the Middle Ages for precision instruments? Talk to James Watt, who, two centuries later, spent thirty years looking in vain for a worker who knew how to produce a more or less circular cylinder for his steam engine. So his machine remained in draft form for three decades for the lack of workers to construct it.

Such was the work of the State in the industrial field. All it could do was to tighten the screw on the worker, depopulate the countryside, sow misery in the towns, reduce millions of people to starvation, impose industrial serfdom.

And it is these pathetic remains of the old guilds, these organisms battered and crushed by the State, these useless cogs of the bureaucracy, which the always 'scientific' economists have in their ignorance confused with the guilds of the Middle Ages. What the Great [French] Revolution swept away as harmful to industry was not the guild, nor even the craft association; it was a useless and harmful cog in the statist machine.

But what the Revolution took great care not to sweep away was the power of the State over industry, over the factory serf.

Do you remember the discussion which took place at the Convention—at the terrible Convention—regarding a strike? To the grievances of the strikers, the Convention replied: 'The State alone has the duty to watch over the interests of all citizens. By striking, you are forming a coalition, you are creating a State within the State. So—death!'

In this reply only the bourgeois nature of the Revolution has been seen. But does it not have a much deeper meaning? Does it not sum up the attitude of the State towards society as a whole, which found its complete and logical expression in the Jacobinism of 1793? 'You have a complaint? Lodge any complaint with the State! It alone has the mission to redress the grievances of its subjects. As for you uniting to defend your-selves—never!' It was in this sense that the Republic was called one and *indivisible*.

Does not the modern Jacobin Socialist think the same? Did not the Convention express the essence of Jacobin thought with the ruthless logic typical of it?

In this reply of the Convention was summed up the atti-tude of all States in regard to all coalitions and all private socie-ties, whatever their aim.

As for the strike, it is still the case that in Russia striking is considered a crime of high treason. To a great extent [this applies] also in Germany, where Wilhelm said to the miners: 'Appeal to me; but if you ever presume to act for yourselves you will know the sabres of my soldiers'.

It is still almost always the case in France. And it is with such a struggle in England[—]after having struggled for a century by [means of] secret societies, by the dagger for trai-tors and for the masters, by explosive powder under machines (as late as 1860), by sand poured into grease boxes [i.e., sabo-tage] and so on[—]that English workers are beginning to win the right to strike, and will soon have it in full—if they do not fall into the traps already set for them by the State, in seeking to impose compulsory arbitration in return for the eight hour law.[33]

---

33 During the 1890s, when Kropotkin was initially writing, there had been massive movements across the industrialised world for an eight-hour workday. He was very impressed by this strike wave and urged Anarchists to take part. However, in 1907, he lamented how this prom-ising movement was side-tracked into electing Socialist politicians who promised to legislate an eight-hour day and, of course, never did; see, respectively, '1st May 1891' and '1886–1907: Glimpses into the Labour Movement in this Country', in *Direct Struggle Against Capital: A Peter Kropotkin Anthology* (Edinburgh: AK Press, 2014). (Editor)

More than a century of terrible struggles! And what misery, with workers dying in prison, transported to Australia, shot, hanged, to regain the right to combine, which—I never tire of repeating this—every man, free or serf, practised freely so long as the State did not lay its heavy hand on societies.

But what! Was it only the worker who was treated in this way?

Let us merely recall the struggles that the bourgeoisie had to wage against the State to win the right to form commercial societies—a right which the State only began to concede when it discovered a convenient means of creating monopolies for the benefit of its creatures and to fill its coffers. Think of the struggles to dare to write, to speak, or even to think otherwise than [the way] the State decrees through the Academy, the University and the Church! Of the struggles that must be waged to this day in order to be able to teach children to read—a right which the State reserves [for itself] but does not use! Of the struggles to even secure the right to have fun together! Not to mention those which would have to be waged in order to dare to choose your judge and your laws—something which was formerly an everyday practice—nor the struggles that will be needed before that book of infamous punishments known as the Penal Code, invented by the spirit of the Inquisition and of the despotic empires of the East, is thrown into the fire!

Observe next taxation—an institution of purely statist origin—this formidable weapon used by the State, in Europe as in the young societies of the two Americas, to keep the masses under its heel, to favour its minions, to ruin the majority for the benefit of the rulers and to maintain the old divisions and the old castes.

Then take the wars, without which States cannot be established nor maintained, wars which become disastrous, inevitable, as soon as it is admitted that a particular region—because it is part of a State—has interests opposed to those of its neighbours who form part of another State. Think of past wars and of those that subjugated people will have to wage to conquer the right to breathe freely; of the wars for markets; of the wars to create colonial empires. And in France we unfortunately know only too well that every war, victorious or not, is followed by slavery.

And finally, what is worse than all that has just been enumerated is that the education we all receive from the State, at school and after, has so corrupted our minds that the very notion of freedom ends up going astray, disguising itself as servitude.

It is a sad sight to see those who believe they are revolutionaries bestow their hatred on the Anarchist—because his concepts of freedom go beyond their petty and narrow notions of freedom learned in the State-controlled school. And yet this spectacle is a reality.

It is because the spirit of voluntary servitude was, and still is, always cleverly cultivated in the minds of the young in order to perpetuate the enslavement of the subject to the State.

Libertarian philosophy is stifled by the Roman and Catholic pseudo-philosophy of the State. History is corrupted from the very first page, where it lies when speaking of the Merovingian and Carolingian monarchies, to the last page where it glorifies Jacobinism and refuses to recognise the role of the people in creating [social] institutions. The natural sciences are perverted, [in order] to be placed at the service of the double idol: Church-State. The psychology of the individual, and even more that of societies, is falsified in each of their assertions to justify the triple alliance of soldier, priest and judge. Finally, morality, after having preached for centuries obedience to the Church or the Book, is today emancipated only to then preach servility to the State: 'No direct moral obligations towards your neighbour, nor even the feeling of solidarity; all your obligations are to the State', we are told, we are taught, in this new cult of the old Roman and Caesarean divinity. 'The neighbour, the comrade, the companion—forget them. You will only know them through the intermediary of some organ of your State. And every one of you will make a virtue of being equally enslaved to it'.

And the glorification of the State and discipline, for which the university and the Church, the press and the political parties work, is propagated so successfully that even revolutionaries dare not face this fetish.

The modern Radical is a centralising statist, an extreme Jacobin. And the Socialist falls into step.[34] Like the Florentines at the end of the fifteenth century who knew no better than to call on the dictatorship of the State to save themselves from the patricians—the Socialists only know to call upon the same gods, the dictatorship of the State, to save themselves from the horrors of the economic regime created by this same State!

X

If we go a little deeper into these diverse categories of facts, which I have scarcely touched upon in this short overview, it will be understood why—seeing the State as it was in history and as it is in its very essence today—and convinced that a social institution cannot lend itself to *all* desired goals since, like every organ, it developed through the function it performed for a definite purpose, not for all possible purposes—it will be understood, I say, why we reach the conclusion of the abolition of the State.

We see in it the institution developed during the history of human societies to prevent the direct association between men,

---

34 As expressed, for example, by Marx in 1850: 'The workers . . . must not only strive for a single and indivisible German republic, but also within this republic for the most determined centralisation of power in the hands of the State authority. They must not allow themselves to be misguided by the democratic talk of freedom for the communities, of self-government, etc. . . . [T]he path of revolutionary activity . . . can proceed with full force only from the centre. . . . As in France in 1793 so today in Germany, it is the task of the really revolutionary party to carry through the strictest centralisation'; *Marx-Engels Collected Works*, vol. 10 (London: Lawrence & Wishart, 1978), 285. (Editor)

to impede the development of local and individual initiative, to crush existing liberties, to prevent their new blossoming—all this [in order] to subjugate the masses to minorities.

And we know that an institution which has a long history dating back several thousand years cannot lend itself to a function opposed to that for which and by which it was developed during the course of history.

To this absolutely unshakeable argument for anyone who has reflected on history—what response do we get?

We are answered with an almost childish argument.

'The State is there', we are told. 'It exists, it represents a powerful ready-made organisation. Why not use it instead of destroying it? It works for evil [ends]—that is true; but that is because it is in the hands of the exploiters. Taken over by the people, why would it not be used for a better purpose, for the good of the people?'

Always the same dream—that of the Marquis de Posa, in Schiller's drama, trying to make absolutism an instrument of emancipation;[35] or else the dream of the gentle Abbé Pierre, in Zola's *Rome*, wanting to make the Church the lever for Socialism![36]

---

35 The Marquis de Posa is a character from Schiller's 1787 play *Don Carlos* (addressing the revolt of the Netherlands against Spanish rule in the sixteenth century) whose famous speech to the King of Spain proclaims Schiller's belief in personal freedom and democracy but ends in a prostrate plea to the King: 'A single word of yours can suddenly/ Create the world anew. Give us the freedom/To think'. (Editor)

36 Abbé Pierre Froment is the hero of Zola's *Three Cities Trilogy*, of which *Rome* (1896) is the second book. In these works, Zola discusses Catholicism, with the hero writing a book to create his 'dream of resuscitating a Christian and evangelical Rome, which should assure the happiness of the world' based on 'a Christian love for the lowly and the wretched'. He visits Rome and meets with the Pope, who promptly rejects the Abbé's vision of a return 'to the spirit of primitive Christianity' and places his work on the index of forbidden books. It ends with denunciations of the Catholic Church and a panegyric to science as sovereign and sweeping all before it. (Editor)

How sad it is to have to answer such arguments! For those who think this way either do not have a clue as to the true historic role of the State or else they understand the *social* revolution in a form so trivial, so anodyne, that it has nothing in common with Socialist aspirations.

Take a concrete example, France.

All those who think must have noticed this striking fact that the Third Republic, in spite of its republican form of government, remained monarchist in its essence. We have all reproached it for not having republicanised France—I am not saying doing nothing for the *social* revolution but of not having even introduced customs—just the *republican* spirit. For the little that has been done for the past twenty-five years to democratise customs or to spread a little education has been done everywhere, in all the European monarchies, under the same pressure of the times we are going through.

So where does the strange anomaly of a republic which remained monarchical come from?

It comes from the fact that France remained a State at the same point that it was thirty years ago. Those holding power have changed the name; but all this immense ministerial scaffolding, all this centralised organisation of bureaucrats, all this imitation of the Rome of the Caesars which has been developed in France, all this formidable organisation to ensure and extend the exploitation of the masses in favour of a few privileged groups that is the essence of the State institution—all that remained. And these cogs [of the bureaucratic machine] continue, as in the past, to exchange their fifty documents when the wind has blown down a tree onto a national highway and to pour the millions deducted from the nation into the coffers of the privileged. The [official] stamp on the documents has changed; but the State, its spirit, its organs, its territorial centralisation, its centralisation of functions, its favouritism, its role as creator of monopolies, have remained. Like an octopus, they expand [their grip] on the country day by day.

The republicans—I speak of the sincere ones—had fuelled the illusion that we could 'utilise the organisation of the State' to produce a change in the republican sense and these are the results. Whereas it was necessary to break the old organisation, *smash the State* and rebuild a new organisation starting with the very foundations of society—the liberated village commune, federalism, groupings from simple to complex, the free workers union—they thought of using the 'organisation that already existed'. And not having understood that we cannot make a historical institution go in the direction that we wish to point it—in the opposite direction to the one it has taken for centuries—they were swallowed up by the institution.

And yet, in this case it was not even a question of changing all the economic relations in society! It was only a question of merely reforming certain aspects of the political relations between men.

But after such a complete failure, in the face of such a sorry experience, they still insist in telling us that the conquest of powers in the State by the people will be sufficient to accomplish the social revolution! That the old machine, the old organisation, slowly developed in the course of history to crush freedom, to crush the individual, to establish oppression on a legal basis, to create monopolists, to lead minds astray by accustoming them to servitude—will lend itself perfectly to new functions: that it will become the instrument, the framework, to germinate a new life, to establish freedom and equality on economic foundations, to eradicate monopolies, to awaken society and march to the conquest of a future of freedom and equality!

What a sad, what a tragic error!

To give full scope to Socialism involves rebuilding from the bottom to the top a society currently based on the narrow individualism of the shopkeeper. It is a question not only— as has sometimes been said by those indulging in vague metaphysics—of giving the worker 'the whole product of his labour'; whereas it is a question of completely reconstructing all relationships, from those which exist today between each individual and his churchwarden or his station-master to those which exist between crafts, hamlets, cities and regions. In every street and hamlet, in every group of men gathered around a factory or along a railway line, it is necessary to awaken the creative, constructive, organisational spirit in order to rebuild all [aspects of] life—in the factory, in the village, in the shop, in production, in distribution. All the relations between individuals and human agglomerations must be rebuilt from the very day, from the very moment, when we lay hands on the current commercial or administrative organisation.

And they want this immense task, which requires the free exercise of the popular genius, to be carried out within the framework of the State, within the organisation's pyramidal ladder that makes the essence of the State! They want the State, whose very reason for existing—as we have seen—is the crushing of the individual, the hatred of initiative, the triumph of *one* idea, which must inevitably be that of mediocrity, to become the lever to accomplish this immense transformation! . . . They want to direct the renewal of a society by means of decrees and electoral majorities . . .

What childishness!

Throughout the history of our civilisation, two traditions, two opposing tendencies, have existed: the Roman tradition and the popular tradition; the imperial tradition and the federalist tradition; the authoritarian tradition and the libertarian tradition.

And once more, on the eve of the social revolution, these two traditions come face to face.

Between these two currents, always living, always in conflict within humanity—the current of the people and the current of minorities thirsting for political and religious domination—we have made our choice.

We continue the one which drove men in the twelfth century to organise on the basis of free agreement, the free initiative of the individual, the free federation of the interested parties. And we leave others to cling to the imperial, Roman and canonical tradition.

History has not been an uninterrupted evolution. On several occasions, [social] evolution has stopped in one region, to start again elsewhere. Egypt, the Middle East, the shores of the Mediterranean, Central Europe were, in turn, the scene of historical development. And every time this evolution begins first with the phase of the primitive tribe, then followed by the village commune, then by the free city, and finally to die in the State phase.

In Egypt, civilisation begins with the primitive tribe. It reaches the village commune, later to the period of free cities; later still, to the State, which, after a period of flourishing, brings—death.

Evolution begins again in Assyria, in Persia, in Palestine. It again passes through the same phases: the tribe, the village commune, the free city, the all-powerful State—death!

A new civilisation then begins in Greece. Still by the tribe. Slowly it reaches the village commune, then the republican cities. In these cities, civilisation reaches its highest peaks. But the East brings its poisonous breath, its traditions of despotism. Wars and conquests create the Empire of Alexander of Macedonia. The State is established, it grows, it kills all civilisation and then—it is death!

Rome in its turn begins civilisation again. It is still the primitive tribe that we find at its origins; then the village commune; then the city. At this phase it reaches the peak of its civilisation. But the State, the Empire, comes and then—death!

On the ruins of the Roman Empire, Celtic, Germanic, Slavic, Scandinavian tribes start civilisation afresh. Slowly the primitive tribe develops its institutions to reach the village commune. It stays in this phase until the twelfth century. Then arises the republican city and this brings the blossoming of the human spirit, expressed by the architectural monuments, the magnificent development of the arts, the discoveries that laid the foundations of natural sciences.... But then comes the State...

Death?

Yes, death—or else renewal! Either the State forever, crushing individual and local life, seizing all areas of human activity, bringing its wars and its internal struggles for the possession of power, its superficial revolutions which only change tyrants and, inevitably, at the end of this evolution—death! Or, States smashed to pieces and a new life starting again in thousands and thousands of centres, on the enduring principle of the initiative of the individual and of groups, on that of free agreement.

Choose!

■ IAIN MCKAY'S BIBLIOGRAPHICAL NOTES TO 'THE STATE: ITS HISTORIC ROLE'

This work was one of the two lectures that Kropotkin never gave, the other being 'Anarchism: Its Philosophy and Its Ideal'.

He had been invited by his friend Jean Grave (1854–1939), the editor of the weekly French anarchist newspaper *Les Temps Nouveaux*, to give two talks as part of a series of lectures on libertarian subjects in Paris that took place in March 1896. However, the heir to the Russian throne decided to visit Nice, where he was to be met by various dignitaries of the French State. Fearing the embarrassment of mass demonstrations in Paris as a result of the crowds Kropotkin would have drawn and the potential damage to the nascent Franco-Russian Alliance, Kropotkin was met by police as he disembarked at Dieppe and forced to return to Britain.

Both talks were turned into pamphlets, and both are libertarian classics. 'Anarchism: Its Philosophy and Its Ideal' was published in France as a pamphlet in 1896 and translated into English the following year, being serialised from July 1896 to March 1897 in *Freedom* and issued as a pamphlet in 1897.[1] 'The State: Its Historic Role' was serialised in *Les Temps Nouveaux* from

---

1   Sadly, the most easily accessible version—in *Anarchism: A Collection of Revolutionary Writings* (Mineola, NY: Dover Books, 2003) and *Fugitive Writings* (Montréal: Black Rose, 1993)—is substantially edited (without indicating so).

19 December to 3 July 1896 in ten not quite weekly parts. It was translated and serialised in *Freedom* from May 1897 to June 1898, and then appeared as a pamphlet in Britain (Freedom Pamphlet no. 11, 1898) long before France (Publications des «Temps nouveaux» no. 33, 1906). In 1913, it was included, slightly revised, as Section III of the last book by Kropotkin published during his lifetime, *La science moderne et l'anarchie*.[2] It was reissued in a new translation by Freedom Press in 1946 (and again in 1968 and 1987) and was included by George Woodcock (1912–1995) in *Fugitive Writings* (Montréal: Black Rose, 1993), volume 10 of Kropotkin's *Collected Works*.

The work is based on the research Kropotkin conducted for what was to become *Mutual Aid* (1902) and draws upon the articles he had written for the journal *The Nineteenth Century*: 'Mutual Aid among Barbarians' (January 1892) and 'Mutual Aid in the Medieval City' (August and September 1894). While the articles and subsequent book were works of popular science directed at a non-anarchist audience, refuting the false assumptions and poor science of Thomas Henry Huxley (1825–1895), 'The State: Its Historic Role' is a much more explicitly anarchist work. This can be seen from its first sentences, which point to the differences between the two schools of socialism—the libertarian and the authoritarian—represented by anarchism and Marxism.

Its aim was to present an evolutionary account of the State, to indicate not only its principal features (i.e., that which makes the State a State) but also *why* it developed such features in the first place. Rather than the metaphysical notions of Marxism (the State simply as an instrument of class rule), he stressed that the State was indeed an instrument of class rule but of *minority* classes. More, its features—centralisation, hierarchy, etc.—did not arise by accident but served this role in society. This meant that the same structure or same features could not

---

2   Now finally available in English as *Modern Science and Anarchy* (Edinburgh: AK Press, 2018). This edition includes a full version of *Anarchism: Its Philosophy and Its Ideal*.

serve different purposes—or social classes—and so rather than the conquest of power by socialists, it would be (to use the title of one Kropotkin's articles) a case of 'The Conquest of Socialists by Power' (*Les Temps Nouveaux*, 21 April 1900).

It is perhaps pointless to add that the twentieth century proved this analysis correct—every Marxist regime quickly became the dictatorship *over* the proletariat, while every social-democratic government at best mitigated but did not end capitalism.

So its overall argument has proven prescient. However, it is not without its issues. Most obviously, as a broad historical account, it can be expected to be sweeping, and while Kropotkin does not present the medieval communes and their institutions completely uncritically, it is fair to say that he does not dwell on their negative aspects. However, given the blind acceptance of Progress (with a capital P) in many circles, he was right to note that we may have lost some things when the rich associational life of the medieval communes was crushed by the rising State and its bureaucracy in the interests of the few. That the American and French Revolutions gave this centralised structure a veneer of popular participation by the masses choosing some of their rulers does not change the fact that the State was transformed into an agent of a *new* minority class, the capitalists.

However, Kropotkin's appreciation of certain elements of medieval Europe did not make him backward looking. It was a case of *learning* from history to inform our struggles today and pointing out that not every social organisation was based on centralised, hierarchical, inevitably bureaucratic forms. People could and had organised—however imperfectly—in *different* ways. And they could again—indeed, every popular revolution has seen the development of community and workplace bodies similar to the medieval commune's quartiers and guilds: the soviets and factory committees of the Russian Revolution, the neighbourhood committees and the better-known workplace and rural collectives of the Spanish Revolution and, most recently, the popular revolt against neo-liberalism in Argentina, which started in December 2001, saw both *autogestión* and *horizontalidad* develop, that is, occupied ('recuperated') workplaces as well as neighbourhood ('barrio') and inter-barrio assemblies. As Kropotkin argued in 1913:

> [T]he State, with its hierarchy of functionaries and the weight of its historical traditions, could only delay the dawning of a new society freed from monopolies and exploitation. . . . [W]hat means can the State provide to abolish this monopoly that the working class could not find in its own strength and groups? . . . [W]hat advantages could the State provide for abolishing these same [class] privileges? Could its governmental machine, developed for the creation and upholding of these privileges, now be used to abolish them? Would not the new function require new organs? And these new organs would they not have to be created by the workers themselves, in *their* unions, *their* federations, completely outside the State?[3]

Thus, the lesson of 'The State: Its Historic Role' remains true—for real change, working-class people need to rely upon and build their *own* organisations and not support or strengthen the structures and forms created to secure their exploitation and oppression. This was something he stressed repeatedly, most notably in Section IV of *La Science Moderne et L'Anarchie*, entitled 'The Modern State'.

Finally, this is a new translation of the revised 1913 edition of Kropotkin's work, based on that of Vernon Richards for the 1968 Freedom Press edition. It first appeared in *Modern Science and Anarchy* (Edinburgh: AK Press, 2018), which also includes a comprehensive set of short biographies of the authors mentioned by Kropotkin.

---

3   Peter Kropotkin, *Modern Science and Anarchy* (Edinburgh: AK Press, 2018), 164.

■ ABOUT THE AUTHORS

Peter Kropotkin (1842–1921) was a Russian revolutionary and geographer, as well as the foremost theorist of the anarchist movement. His classic works include *The Conquest of Bread*; *Fields, Factories and Workshops*; *Memoirs of a Revolutionist*; *Mutual Aid*; and the essays contained in this collection.

Brian Morris, professor emeritus at Goldsmiths College, University of London, has written extensively in the fields of botany, ecology, ethnobiology, religion, history, philosophy and anthropology. His many books include *Kropotkin: The Politics of Community* and *Anthropology, Ecology, and Anarchism: A Brian Morris Reader*.

Iain McKay is an independent anarchist writer and researcher. He was the main author of *An Anarchist FAQ*, as well as numerous other works, including *Mutual Aid: An Introduction and Evaluation*. In addition, he edited and introduced *Property Is Theft! A Pierre-Joseph Proudhon Anthology*; *Direct Struggle Against Capital: A Peter Kropotkin Anthology*; and Kropotkin's 1913 book *Modern Science and Anarchy*. He has also written for *Freedom*, *Black Flag* and *Anarcho-Syndicalist Review*.

ABOUT PM PRESS

PM Press was founded at the end of 2007 by a small collection of folks with decades of publishing, media, and organizing experience. PM Press co-conspirators have published and distributed hundreds of books, pamphlets, CDs, and DVDs. Members of PM have founded enduring book fairs, spearheaded victorious tenant organizing campaigns, and worked closely with bookstores, academic conferences, and even rock bands to deliver political and challenging ideas to all walks of life. We're old enough to know what we're doing and young enough to know what's at stake.

We create radical and stimulating fiction and non-fiction books, pamphlets, T-shirts, visual and audio materials to educate, entertain, and inspire you. We aim to distribute these through every available channel with every available technology—whether that means you are seeing anarchist classics at our bookfair stalls; reading our latest vegan cookbook at the café; downloading geeky fiction e-books; or digging new music and timely videos from our website.

PM Press is always on the lookout for talented and skilled volunteers, artists, activists, and writers to work with. If you have a great idea for a project or can contribute in some way, please get in touch.

PM Press
PO Box 23912
Oakland, CA 94623
www.pmpress.org

FRIENDS OF PM PRESS

These are indisputably momentous times—the financial system is melting down globally and the Empire is stumbling. Now more than ever there is a vital need for radical ideas.

In the seven years since its founding—and on a mere shoestring—PM Press has risen to the formidable challenge of publishing and distributing knowledge and entertainment for the struggles ahead. With over 300 releases to date, we have published an impressive and stimulating array of literature, art, music, politics, and culture. Using every available medium, we've succeeded in connecting those hungry for ideas and information to those putting them into practice.

Friends of PM allows you to directly help impact, amplify, and revitalize the discourse and actions of radical writers, filmmakers, and artists. It provides us with a stable foundation from which we can build upon our early successes and provides a much-needed subsidy for the materials that can't necessarily pay their own way. You can help make that happen—and receive every new title automatically delivered to your door once a month—by joining as a Friend of PM Press. And, we'll throw in a free T-shirt when you sign up.

Here are your options:

- **$30 a month** Get all books and pamphlets plus 50% discount on all webstore purchases

- **$40 a month** Get all PM Press releases (including CDs and DVDs) plus 50% discount on all webstore purchases

- **$100 a month** Superstar—Everything plus PM merchandise, free downloads, and 50% discount on all webstore purchases

For those who can't afford $30 or more a month, we're introducing **Sustainer Rates** at $15, $10 and $5. Sustainers get a free PM Press T-shirt and a 50% discount on all purchases from our website.

Your Visa or Mastercard will be billed once a month, until you tell us to stop. Or until our efforts succeed in bringing the revolution around. Or the financial meltdown of Capital makes plastic redundant. Whichever comes first.

Kropotkin: The Politics of Community

Brian Morris

$24.95
ISBN: 978-1-62963-505-7
6x9 • 320 pages

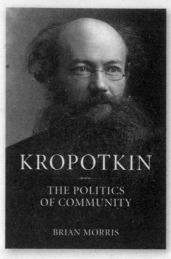

The nineteenth century witnessed the growth of anarchist literature, which advocated a society based on voluntary cooperation without government authority. Although his classical writings on mutual aid and the philosophy of anarchism are still published today, Peter Kropotkin remains a neglected figure. A talented geographer and a revolutionary socialist, Kropotkin was one of the most important theoreticians of the anarchist movement.

In *Kropotkin: The Politics of Community*, Brian Morris reaffirms with an attitude of critical sympathy the contemporary relevance of Kropotkin as a political and moral philosopher and as a pioneering social ecologist. Well-researched and wide-ranging, this volume not only presents an important contribution to the history of anarchism, both as a political tradition and as a social movement, but also offers insightful reflections on contemporary debates in political theory and ecological thought. After a short biographical note, the book analyzes in four parts Kropotkin's writings on anarchist communism, agrarian socialism, and integral education; modern science and evolutionary theory; the French Revolution and the modern state; and possessive individualism, terror, and war.

Standing as a comprehensive and engaging introduction to anarchism, social ecology, and the philosophy of evolutionary holism, *Kropotkin* is written in a straightforward manner that will appeal to those interested in social anarchism and in alternatives to neoliberal doctrines.

"Peter Kropotkin has been largely ignored as a utopian crackpot, but Brian Morris demonstrates in this wide-ranging and detailed analysis that Kropotkin addressed significantly and perceptively the major issues of the present day."
—Harold B. Barclay, author of *People without Government: An Anthropology of Anarchy*